A Life Well Lived

Biography of Tina Petkau

Beverly Wiebe

DEDICATION

I want to dedicate this book to my dad as well as all of my sisters and brothers, Alice, Maria, Elizabeth, Gertrude, Clara, Doris, Doreen, Tina, Henry, Janice, Sara, Melvin, Loyd, Darlene and Bernice, if mom could say something to all of us again, I think she would once again say these familiar words, "Never, ever give up! Keep on keeping on, heaven will be worth it all."

Henry and Tina and their children

CONTENTS

ACKNOWLEDGMENTS

There are so many people I'd like to thank, the first of them being my mom. Thank you so much mom for showing me how to love the Lord. Thank you for the endless hours of story telling and information gathering you did to make this book possible. I wish I could have finished writing it before you passed away so that you could have read it. You lived an amazing life and it is a story worth sharing.

Thank you Johnny for your support and encouragement through it all and Donnovin, Ana and Jared for all your help. Thank you for believing in me and cheering me on.

Thank you dad and siblings for sharing your stories as well as being ready to gather information when I needed it.

I also want to thank all my friends and family that have encouraged me.

Most of all, thank you Heavenly Father for blessing me with such a wonderful mom, the best mom in the world!

Preface

Many years ago Tina, my mom, asked me to make a note that would be
kept in a safe place. She wanted the gospel to be shared with everyone at
her funeral. She knew that there would be a lot of people there and her
desire was for everyone to hear about Salvation, God's greatest gift to us,
through the birth, death and resurrection of Jesus. Tina passed away in
March of 2020, right at the onset of Covid, which was also the most
restrictive time for gathering together. As a result, her funeral was very
small, with mostly family in attendance. This meant that not many people
were able to hear the message she had wanted proclaimed. In addition to
the note she had asked me to write, we also found the note below, kept in a
safe place, after she passed away.

I have written this book to honour my mom's request and to tell her
story.

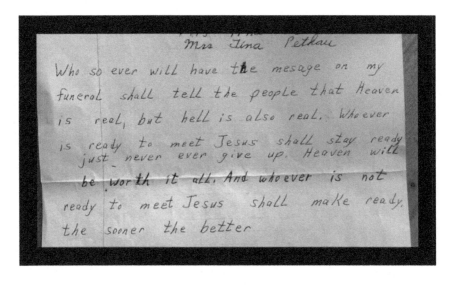

1 THE EARLY YEARS

I've often heard people say that they have or had the 'best mom'. As much as I know that there are and have been many amazing, godly moms out there, you will have to forgive me when I say that I truly believe that I, in fact, had the best mom to ever exist...simply because she was mine! This is her story....

On April 11, 1938, Tina was born into a committed Christian-Mennonite family. She was the eleventh in a family of seventeen children. Her parents, Henry and Elizabeth Plett were humble, hardworking farmers, as well as business owners. They lived on a modest farm in the Canadian prairies just outside the small village of Hanover, Manitoba. The springs were cool and the summers short and busy, followed by the arrival of vast expanses of golden fields, ripe to harvest in the fall. Once harvested, the Plett's would settle in for the long, bitter, cold winters, winters so long they tried the spirits of even the most patient people.

Those early years of life were good for little Tina. She was surrounded by parents and siblings that loved her and the Lord. Her home was a safe place where the value of hard work and devotion to God were highly prized. There may not have been much laughter in the home, as the seriousness of life was always before them, but there was peace and contentment in the Plett household despite the difficulties.

Tina was a happy and content little girl. She cheerfully did the tasks assigned her only to return to her toys and the world of playing pretend. She remained blissfully unaware of the difficulties that her family struggled through during the last years they spent in Manitoba.

Many modern medical advancements had not appeared in their part of the world at the time, so for large families to occasionally lose a baby in infancy was quite common. Two of Tina's siblings passed away at a young age and one other sister, Shirley, suffered brain damage from a fall. As a result of this injury, Shirley spent the remainder of her life needing help with nearly everything she did. All these events happened within a couple years of each other and were very hard on the whole family, especially for Tina's mom. She carried a deep concern for her handicapped daughter and worried about Shirley being able to receive the care and love that she would need when the time came that she, as a mother, could no longer take care of her daughter. Although Tina's mom may have at times forgotten how to laugh due to the hardships of life, she did have a heart full of peace and showed kindness to all who knew her.

Tina and her siblings spent many hours every day playing inside the house and out on their farm with their simple toys, which included sticks and stones and old scraps of garbage. Their play time was often interrupted by their mother calling them to do chores. All the children were expected to do their part, no exceptions. There was so much work around the farm that even the youngest of them wasn't left out. Oftentimes they would forget that they were working, as jobs became games they would play.

Of course, on Saturdays the house had to be cleaned from top to bottom in preparation for Sunday. Everyone had to help with this task, not just the girls but the boys as well, which was not as common in most Mennonite homes. This particular morning Tina's job was to sweep and mop the floor and, once again, this turned into something fun to do. She waited until the house was quiet, which meant everyone except her mom had gone outside. That's exactly how Tina liked it.

Tina filled the mop bucket with hot, soapy water and started mopping the floor. She made sure that the mop was dripping wet every time she lifted it out of the bucket. She did this again and again until the smooth concrete floor was glistening wet. This meant it was perfect! Tina glanced over at her mom, who was doing some mending in the next room. She noticed that her mom kept her head down, continuing with her mending and paying no attention to her or what she was doing.

With a slight smile on her face, Tina began to gingerly slide across the slippery floor in her bare feet. It was wonderful but it needed a bit more soap. Another squirt and the floor became even slipperier. Back and forth she slid, right past the door where her mom was sitting. Her mother remained busy and pretended not to notice what was going on. It was great fun! Warm, soapy water on a smooth concrete floor made for a perfect "slip n' slide" surface. Cleaning the floor this way made it fun and Tina nearly forgot that she was doing a task. After she landed on the floor again, Tina finished mopping then walked outside to join the others. She knew that her mom would keep her secret safe.

The following day, Sunday, they went to the little country church down the road. Sunday was the highlight of the week. She loved going to church to see all her friends. After church they would most likely have friends or family over to their house for dinner or for *faspa* later that day. *Faspa* was a light traditional Mennonite meal that was reserved for Sundays and holidays. It was eaten at 4:30 in the afternoon and consisted of homemade bread and buns, butter, fruit preserves, cheese, and cookies or cake.

Weekends were wonderful, but for Tina, Mondays were equally wonderful! She would get up early, along with her older siblings, and get ready to go to the little, private, Christian school in Hanover, which was the nearest town to where they lived. Tina loved school; all the writing and arithmetic was fun and came easily to her. She was often one of the first ones to be done with her work and would then be able to draw or color a picture the teacher would give her. Working extra hard at making her handwriting look very neat and tidy was also satisfying for her.

Friday was the best day of the week, not because it was the last day of school, but it was the day they had art class, the last class of the week. Although the assignments were simple and not considered a real subject, they were a treat and Tina looked forward to them every week. Tina very quickly developed a real love for creating beautiful art, a hobby and talent that she carried with her throughout her whole life.

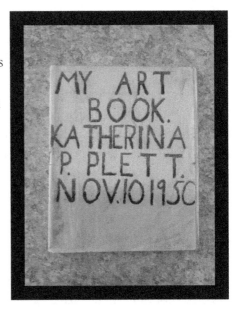

When Tina was ten years old, there was much pressure from the governing authorities in Manitoba to close all private Christian schools and make attending public schools mandatory for children. Tina's parents had always seen great value in being able to provide their children with a solid, Christian education. Now they were faced with the possibility that private education would no longer be an option. They also struggled with the fear that their sons might be drafted, as was common during the recently fought World War II. As a result, they made the decision to move the family down to Mexico.

In Mexico, most of the small Mennonite *colonies,* had their own private schools run by their churches. As a result, these schools remained free from outside interference. These *colonies* were essentially small farming communities occupied exclusively by Mennonites. The people in these *colonies* kept very much to themselves, occasionally going out and visiting other similar *colonies.* The Mennonites prided themselves on their self-sufficiency. They had their own stores, restaurants, and hospitals for basic health care needs. Only on rare occasions did they require trips to outside towns or cities. The possibility of living in a community like that appealed to the Plett family, especially when it came down to how much influence the government would have on their lives. After much discussing and consulting, preparations for the move began.

The first order of business for them would be to sell the family business. Henry Plett, Tina's father, had begun a small business in Manitoba, making cheese boxes for the large round cheeses that were common at the time. Over the years, the business had done well and had grown to employ numerous family members as well as other people from their community. The cheese boxes became popular and were being sold and shipped across the province. As the president of the company, Tina's father sat in the office making all the deals happen and keeping the whole operation running smoothly. Now it was also his job to find a buyer for the business, which would inevitably allow their family to leave the area.

On October 16, 1948, the journey to Mexico began. There was no large U-haul truck or trailer that accompanied the family on their move across the continent. It was a simple truck with a trailer and a camper that covered the back. Attached to the camper was a rustic, makeshift flatbed camper trailer hitched at the very back, which was lovingly referred to as the "Caboose". The floor of the flatbed camper was covered with numerous mattresses, sponges, and blankets that the children could sit on while they traveled. The "Caboose" also had a spot for sleeping, which was where the parents

5

slept at night. It also contained many boxes and other belongings that the family was moving with them, some of which needed to be placed outside at night to expand the sleeping space. They spread out as much bedding as possible, covering the floors of both trailers. Despite this, the space was still limited and every night some of the older children took their bedding outside and laid it on the grass.

The 'Caboose'

The trip down to Mexico took a little over three weeks. Throughout the duration of the journey, the Plett's along with an additional couple that traveled with them, never slept in a hotel, or ate at restaurants. Instead, the ingredients were purchased in grocery stores and the meals were prepared at rest areas on a homemade gas stove that they had brought with them. Not only did this save them a lot of money, but also gave the younger children time to run and play which was a much-needed break from travel.

On November 6, 1948, the weary family arrived on the little farm property in Mexico with nothing more than the clothes on their backs and the few household items they had brought with them on their trip. It was late in the afternoon by the time the truck came to its final stop and the whole family piled out, eager to see their new home. The driveway they had pulled into led right up to what was presumably the house, even though it was the saddest looking building on the yard. Numerous sections of peeling paint exposed the weathered wood underneath and a couple of broken windows caused the building to look more like a barn than a house. To call this building a town house would have been entirely too kind, but that was the general design. It was a rectangular building that had been divided into three sections, all having an outside door and only one room inside.

Beyond the house, there were several small buildings situated throughout the property such as a few sheds and an old, red barn. Scattered across the yard were several leafless trees casting their long shadows across the sparse, dry, brown grass that had gone to sleep for the winter months. It was hard for the Plett's to believe the home before them would house their own large family as well as two other families, which consisted of Tina's aunts and their husbands. They had all known ahead of time that when they got to Mexico their living standards would be downgraded but this was even rougher than they had imagined.

Tina was tired, hot, and hungry, but instead of running into the house, her curiosity drove her to hop out of the back of the truck and do a quick tour of the new little farm.

Excitedly, she ran around the yard. She had been hoping that they would be able to have a lot of different farm animals, and it looked to her like there would be enough space for that. After having explored enough to satisfy her immediate curiosity, Tina headed back to where the rest of the family was. She felt quite excited at the thought of all the possibilities.

When Tina got into the house, her dad was already explaining how he would be able to make this little, one room house fit his large family. He planned to make a partial second floor over a portion of the home. This upper portion of the house would be big and high enough to place mattresses on the floor where most of the children would sleep. A ladder would be built and fastened onto one side of the house to make access to the second floor easy and convenient. This would take some time to finish so, for tonight, they would have to come up with another solution that might not be as comfortable.

As Tina stood in the door of the house, looking unimpressed at what was before her. She looked down at the floor and saw what appeared to be patches of old, dried-up cow manure. Thankfully, there were no fresh messes that she could see, but still the flies were terrible! They were everywhere, buzzing about them. Tina could not imagine being able to sleep peacefully in this place. She blurted out the first thing that came to her mind.

"Is this a house or is it a barn, dad?" She walked in and looked up at him. "It really stinks in here," she continued.

"This will be our home," her father declared, matter-of-factually.

"But I really don't want to sleep here," Tina continued.

After some time of looking around and sharing ideas on how to spend the night, Tina stepped back outside and noticed that her parents were quietly talking beside the truck, neither of them looking happy. Evening was quickly approaching and it would be dark soon. It was decided that for tonight, they would use the same sleeping arrangements that they had been utilizing while traveling. Supper also needed to be made so there would be no time to clean the house enough for anyone to sleep inside.

The next couple of days were a frantic frenzy of cleaning, building, and unpacking, while at the same time taking care of the big family. With her sister Shirley and baby brother Timmy, who was sick, requiring so much care, Tina was too young to realize how hard this whole transition was on her parents and older siblings.

However, being ten years old, Tina was still a big help. She would cook, clean, and took care of her younger siblings. She especially enjoyed holding Timmy, the baby, but lately, as she held her baby brother, she felt sad. He didn't seem to be getting better and, sadly, just two weeks after arriving in Mexico, Timmy passed away.

The weeks leading up to Christmas that year were sad and lonely, a hard beginning to their life in Mexico. Even though they didn't have their own church yet, the family went and joined the local Mexicans in their little village for church on Sundays. They didn't know Spanish and could not understand what was being said. Despite that, they received much encouragement from church as well as from singing together as a family on Sunday afternoons.

Strong family relationships were also developed and strengthened during those early years in Mexico. Numerous of Tina's uncles and aunts also lived nearby and one way they would help each other was with doing a combined family grocery shopping trip. About once a month, one of the brothers would call and get all the siblings orders for flour, sugar, and a few other items that they needed from the local grocery store. He would then go purchase the items and deliver them to everyone's house.

It was on that little farm that Tina fell in love with farming. She quickly discovered that she loved working in the fields and taking care of the animals. Her keen interest in this made her the one who would mainly take care of the chickens that her parents purchased.

Although the family started out with only a small number of chickens, it didn't take long before Tina was taking care of a couple thousand chickens at a time. Everyday there would be many eggs to gather and, once gathered, any of her siblings who had time would help clean them. All the eggs had to be wiped, washed, and sorted. Cracked eggs were kept on a separate crate, which was brought inside to be eaten by the family. All the remaining clean, white eggs were carefully stacked for the ride into town where they would be sold.

Tina would calculate how much money it would take to feed and raise the chickens. She soon learned how long the chickens needed to lay eggs until they had paid for themselves and at what point her parents could expect to start making a monetary profit on them. Tina kept a small notebook out in the barn where she would keep track of all the expenses as well as the money earned from selling eggs. Tina loved it! Combining her love of farming with her mathematical mind was very rewarding to her.

Then there were some jobs that nobody enjoyed doing. The worst of them was working out in the fields at night. It was a lonely job and one that filled her heart with fear, but this night it was Tina's turn. By the time she walked outside to the barn and got the tractor going, the sun was already setting and darkness was quickly approaching. There was the constant fear of thieves, wild animals, and even the simple fear of being in the dark that most girls her age would agree was terrifying. Tina's fears kept her on the alert and looking over her shoulder constantly. It also motivated her to convince one of her younger sisters to go with her. So, while the world around her went to sleep and the sister beside Tina closed her eyes and rested her head on her older sister's shoulder, young Tina courageously faced her fears and worked the fields.

A couple of years later when Tina was a little older, around twelve or thirteen, taking care of the cattle also became one of the things that was required of her. Tina, along with one or two of her sisters, would round up their family's cattle and herd them down the main street that went through the center of their little village and beyond. The summers were long, hot, and dry and, by the time July or August came, most farmers looked beyond their farms into the surrounding meadows in hopes of finding some green grass for their livestock to graze on.

Clouds of dust billowing and rising in the air from the hooves of running cattle and the young, barefoot girls with long sticks in their hands walking down the dirt road through town, served as an announcement to the surrounding neighbors that someone was taking cattle to the pastures out of town. Often, Tina and her sister would be met by some other farmers who would ask them to watch their herds for the day. These days were normally somewhat boring and uneventful. The girls would find things to talk about, pick some flowers, or would simply sit quietly, watching the cattle, always ready to gently round up the ones that were straying a little too far away. Tina was calm and gentle, never loud, or hasty. She knew that the cattle could sense her emotions and would respond much better if everyone remained calm and unhurried.

The fear of potential thieves was constant in the girls' minds. It was not uncommon for thieves to come with their horses and round up some of the cattle that belonged to the Mennonites and simply take them away. After all, what would the defenseless farmers, who believed that they should not fight back, do if approached by an armed robber?

While they hadn't seen or experienced anything like this for themselves, they had heard many stories of others in their Mennonite community who had been robbed, hurt, or frightened by the Mexican bandits that roamed the area. Tina had no idea what she would do if this ever happened to her and her sisters while they were out on their own. Thankfully she never had to find out, but that didn't mean it wasn't a frequent fear of theirs. On occasion they would spot a horse and rider in the distance and fear would once again grip their hearts until the rider would eventually disappear into the distance.

Although they had never been bothered while out with the cattle, they had not been as fortunate at home. Over the years, there were numerous times that a group of bandits had come riding to their front door, dismounted and forced their way into their home. Every time this happened the demands were the same "Give us your money and no one will get hurt!"

Tina's dad really didn't want to give his hard-earned money away, so, in an act of bravery, he would always offer them food instead. Initially, the thieves would get angry, but the food would eventually appease them and they would leave soon afterwards.

During their time out on the pasture and on the farm, Tina and her sisters learned to tell time. Near the end of the day, Tina would hold her hand up against the sun to measure how much farther it needed to drop before it would slip behind the distant mountains. As soon as the gap between the sun and the distant horizon was only a hands width apart, the girls knew that it was time to gather the cattle and head back home.

The next day there would be someone else taking the cattle out and for Tina there would be some other job. This was one of the benefits of being in a large family where many tasks needed to get done. Besides the farming, there was also a garden that always needed attention. It got a little bigger every year and at the end of the summer there was always a lot of harvesting to be done. The family did not own a freezer, so the garden vegetables were mostly canned so that they would last them through the winter. Potatoes, carrots, and other root vegetables were put in their cold cellar to stay fresh enough to eat until the following spring or early summer.

Tina felt happy as she worked alongside her older sister, digging potatoes out of the garden. They had a huge crop this year and Tina was excited to show her mom and dad all the potatoes they had spread out on the grass. Tina's older sister was happy too. She was happy because she would be able to stay home, unlike Tina who was happy because she could go back to school the next day.

Tina loved school! She loved books and all the new things she would learn. School also gave her the opportunity to spend a little more time with friends and that was always fun.

The next morning, Tina was up bright and early once again. She slipped out of bed and tiptoed over to the chair in the corner of the room. Over the chair hung her one and only school dress. It was a simple dress, nothing fancy about it, but it was new and the bright flowers on the black background were beautiful. For Tina, a new dress was always exciting. She did not often get a new piece of clothing. In fact, most of her clothes were hand-me-downs from her older sisters. She never had more than two or three dresses at any given time, which was a big reason why this morning was so special. It was the first day of the new school year and Tina would be able to go to school in a pretty, new dress.

Breakfast was eaten, lunches were made, and then it was time to head out to school. Tina and her younger siblings ran out and hopped up into the manure spreader that their father had cleaned and hitched up to one of their horses. The same manure spreader that had been previously used to work in the fields was now being used as a ride to school.

School was close to their home, only a couple miles down the road, and most days they would walk there and back but today, they had a ride. Tina was the oldest present and, immediately, took charge of handling the horse and directing it. As soon as they arrived at school, Tina placed the reins over the horse's neck and gave it a gentle slap on the rump along with a firm, "Go home" command. The horse promptly turned around and trotted back home, where their dad would be ready to unhitch her from the manure spreader and put her back to pasture again.

Tina was in grade eight this year, which would most likely be the last year of school for her. Anyone who was able to finish grade eight was considered fortunate. In the minds of most of the Mennonites at that time, there was no need for a high school education, and even the teaching in the elementary school years were often lacking. The teachers often did not have a good understanding of what they were teaching as they themselves lacked a good education. It was not a job that was given much respect and often it was people who couldn't find a job elsewhere that would end up being teachers. As a result, the basics to learning how to read, write and do simple math was taught, but beyond that there was not much importance placed on education.

That was also the year that Tina started to have a 'secret admirer' who would sometimes show up around school. At first, she didn't notice it, but eventually it did become increasingly obvious, and she was no longer the only one to take note.

On one warm, sunny day in April, the students were eating their lunches outside under the shade trees in the school yard. After lunch, the children joined in a game of soccer. Tina loved playing sports at school and was quite focused on the game until one of her friends tapped her on the shoulder.

"Tina, look. That horse and buggy has ridden past the school at least three times already."

Tina looked, and sure enough, she did recognize the young man in the buggy. It was Henry Petkau, a teenager from the little village just three kilometers down the road from her house.

"I think he's looking at you Tina," her friend continued.

"Oh, stop it!" Tina whispered, even though she believed it was true. "Let's just keep playing," Tina insisted, even as she felt her face growing warm, knowing it must be getting red from embarrassment.

Henry was a popular, good-looking guy, and could have had his pick of pretty much any girl in the area, but his heart was set on Tina. His parents had bought a new buggy the day before so, naturally, Henry had hitched it up to their best horse and taken it for a ride into the village to hopefully catch a glimpse of Tina at school.

Luckily, he had timed it just right and his efforts had been rewarded with a sight that he never forgot his whole life: a beautiful, teenage girl, running barefoot in her new, floral black dress, playing a game of soccer with her friends. A more beautiful sight he had never seen and that was the day he knew that he wanted to spend the rest of his life with her, the pretty girl from Grehnlant who always seemed to have a smile on her face.

Tina(right) and one of her sisters

2 TIMES WERE TIGHT

Bright and early on a cold, winter morning in 1955, Tina in her simple, black dress, walked down the street to the colony's Mennonite church, along with numerous other young people from her youth group. Slowly and solemnly, the ladies led the group inside where they walked to the front of the church, sitting on the cold, wooden pews. Walking behind them were the young men who sat opposite them on the other side of the aisle. One of these young men was Henry Petkau, the young man who fancied Tina and her delightful smile. Once seated, the only sound to be heard was that of a fire crackling in the back of the one room building.

The service proceeded as usual. Hymns were sung without any musical accompaniment, followed by an opening devotional and then the sermon. The service was done in German, both High and Low which was common in many Mennonite churches. The only difference in today's service was that once the sermon was completed, everyone turned their attention to the young people sitting in the front.

This was a very important day for them, it was the day that they were going to be baptized upon their profession of faith, and at the same time be accepted into the membership of the church. It was not a long baptism ceremony; the minister got right to the point.

The method of teaching foundational truths of the faith in a question-and-answer format was used, also known as Catechism.

Tina quietly answered every single one of the questions in her mind. She couldn't help but feel quite pleased with herself for having all of it perfectly memorized. Tina loved memorizing verses as well as other writings and was very quick at doing so. Over the past number of weeks, she had carefully recited all the answers to the questions over and over to herself or to anyone else who would listen to her.

When the catechism questions were completed, the minister asked them to kneel on the floor in front of their seats, with heads bowed in patient anticipation. He then stepped in front of each one of them and reverently raised his little plastic pitcher and poured a little bit of water on their heads, thus baptizing them in the name of the Father, the Son, and the Holy Ghost. He shook their hands as he helped them to their feet and the youth were presented as members of the church.

A couple of months after their baptism, on June seventeenth, shortly after Tina's eighteenth birthday, she married Henry. They promised to be faithful to each other in sickness and in health, for better or for worse, and to love each other until death would part them. There isn't much to say about Tina and Henry's courtship except that it lasted all of one year with marriage as the end goal. The couple would see each other at church gatherings or at friends' homes and had a few dates from time to time. During these dates, Henry would come see Tina and they would sit and talk for a few hours about anything; usually there would be people at home so their dates would be, in a way, supervised from a distance. During the course of a courtship period a watch was very often gifted to the girl by the boyfriend. This was the custom in the Mennonite community during that time instead of engagement or wedding rings.

The wedding ceremony was a very simple service that was performed immediately following the Sunday morning church service. Henry and Tina were invited to come sit in the very front of the sanctuary along with any other couples who also wanted to get married that Sunday. The service consisted of vows being exchanged between each of the couples followed by a serious sermon on the duties and difficulties of marriage.

Following the service their families and friends would share a simple *faspa* of sandwiches and cookies that had been prepared by the families the day before.

After the *faspa*, Henry and Tina drove straight to their new home. They did not have the luxury of a wedding trip or getting any time off from work. The next day Henry would be back at work like any other Monday morning. They pulled into the Petkau parents' driveway and drove up to a rustic, one room house that was situated on the same property as Henry's old home. The tiny 10-by-10 shack had previously

Henry and Tina's Wedding Day

served as a bedroom for two of Henry's older brothers since the main family home was also quite small. Earlier that day, the brothers had moved their things out and allowed Henry and Tina to live there until they could find a place of their own.

Less than a year later, Henry and Tina welcomed their first baby girl into their lives, and she was the first of many to come. Over the next twenty years, sixteen children would be born into the Petkau family, thirteen girls and three boys. Unfortunately, Tina would also experience grief just as her mother had, going through three miscarriages during this time.

What a gift from God it was that Tina's mom was able to be a midwife and, as a result, was able to assist Tina with the birth of her first children. God's blessing was truly felt as Tina was able to give birth to all those little ones naturally, with no medical intervention. There was even a set of twins and what a surprise that had been! In all those years, Tina had only been in active labor for a total of fifty hours! That worked out to a little over three hours of labor per birth.

Tina's mother was very pleased to have so many grandchildren and she loved being a grandma to each one of them. She was a gentle lady and was widely known for her compassionate heart and caring nature. She was one of the local midwives but also had other nursing duties that she cheerfully preformed at the little clinic in their colony. When new mothers would come in with their babies, she was the one who would administer their immunization shots. However, this was something that she refused to do to her own grandchildren to the inconvenience of Tina that morning.

"Mom, why won't you give my little girls their shots?" Tina once again questioned her mom when she stopped in at the clinic.

Tina had gone into the clinic that day hoping to have two of her little girls get their immunizations but if her mother was the only one there Tina knew she would have to come back again another day.

"Really it would be much more convenient if you would just do it instead of me having to wait and come back another day," Tina tried to reason with her mother.

"Tina, I'm sorry but I really don't want to poke my grand babies. I don't ever want them to associate me with a painful experience."

Her mother patted Tina on the shoulder as she handed one of the little girls back to her.

"I just want to hold and hug your girls," her mother said as they walked toward the door. "Come back tomorrow and someone else will be here."

As Tina and her girls prepared to leave, her mother knelt down in front of two year old Tara. "Come, Tara." She reached out her hands to the young child. "Let me look at your forehead."

Tara eagerly ran over to her grandma, pushed the stray hair away from her forehead, excited to show her grandma how much better she was.

"Look, grandma, it's all better," she happily declared.

"Yes, I think you are right. It looks as if it is indeed almost all better." Grandma said as she ran her hand over the little girls' forehead and noticed that it was nearly smooth.

Earlier that month Tina had been outside with her girls, cleaning up around the chicken coup while the girls were playing outside.

"Mamma, I'm hungry," Tara called out as she poked her head

through the open window of the coup to see where her mom was working. She was hardly tall enough to look through the window, so she jumped up and pulled herself onto the windowsills edge, balancing precariously on her tummy while gripping the edge of the sill so as not to fall. "Mamma, look at me!" Tara exclaimed.

Tina turned just in time to see her little daughter loose her hold on the windowsill's edge and come crashing headfirst onto the graveled floor beneath her. Immediately, Tara started crying. Tina hurried over to her and scooped her up into her arms. Her forehead was already covered in blood. The soft skin of the young girl was no match for the small, sharp pebbles on the ground.

"Shh, Tara," Tina's voice broke as she tried to remain calm while attempting to comfort her wailing child. She had never been good at handling blood, let alone when it involved one of her little girls. "Oh dear, what will I do?" She whispered softly under her breath while her mind raced.

Tina's hands shook as she gently wiped the blood from her little girls face to get a better look at the damage. The blood kept flowing and Tina was unable to see much of anything. She quickly pulled the clean handkerchief from her pocket and held it gingerly against her daughter's head to keep the blood from dripping into her eyes. She prayed quietly under her breath, "God please help me! Please help me to know what to do."

She could see that there were several tiny stones that had gotten lodged in the cuts on Tara's forehead; they would have to be taken out, so they could be cleaned.

"Don't cry Tara," Tina tried to sooth the sobbing girl. "I think we should go see grandma," she decided. Tara was quieting down a little by then and rested her cheek on her mother's shoulder. "Let's go see if grandma can help you." Tina looked down and smiled reassuringly at her. "You always like going to grandma's house, Tara, don't you?" The two of them had then walked over to Grandma's house where Tina's mom had lovingly and patiently removed all the little pebbles from Tara's face.

Fast forward to three weeks later as they were leaving the clinic, the grandmother's inspection of the child's' face led to the conclusion that it was nearly back to normal. Remembering how her mother had helped in such a scary situation, Tina felt a sense of thankfulness for her mother's kindness.

She smiled and said, "Okay, mom. I'll come back tomorrow. Thank you for caring for your grandchildren and loving them the same."

She walked out the door with her little girls in tow.

On most days, Tina would put the children to bed early and then she would have some much-needed quiet time to get a few things done. Often, these hours were used for sewing, the way that Tina had been able to help contribute to the financial well-being of the family. The sewing she did was for some of the wealthier people in town who would ask her to sew clothes for them. They would bring over lovely fabrics for her to work with.

Once she would get paid for her work they would use the hard-earned money to buy groceries. She would then re-use the packaging the groceries were in to make clothes for her family. The large flour sacks were made of rough brown or white fabric, from which she would make dresses for the girls. These clothes were not beautiful or colorful in any way, but they were strong and didn't cost any extra money. Tina loved quiet evenings of sewing and found it to be a relaxing and enjoyable way to end the day.

Most mornings, Tina was up bright and early, just as the sun started to peek out from behind the distant hills. A low fog was dissipating as she looked out from the front door of their one room home on that cool November morning.

Tina had slept well, and her five girls were still sleeping. She gazed at the peaceful faces of the girls laying on the floor in the corner of the room while the baby slept quietly in the crib next to her bed.

The home was tiny and sparsely furnished, a bed for Henry and Tina and a small area for the girls to sleep. On the opposite wall was their meager kitchen which contained the bare necessities. The floor and the walls were made of concrete that was neither smooth nor painted. There was no running water and the only bathroom they had was an outhouse at the back of the house

It was going to be a busy day, as all of them were, so that was nothing new. Henry was gone on the truck again and Tina had no idea when he was going to be back. He had left a couple days ago to bring a load of farm machinery from America to Mexico and she had no way of communicating with him. He would often be gone on these trips for days or even a week or two at a time.

Today was laundry day and Tina wanted to get an early start since the most productive hours of the day were the ones before the girls woke up. She took one last glance over at the sleeping girls before she carefully opened the door and quietly slipped outside. She pulled her sweater tightly around herself as a cool breeze gently tugged at her dress. It was quiet and peaceful as she walked across the back yard and into the pasture behind their home. She had hoped that Henry might take the time to get some firewood for her before leaving on one of his business trips again, but it had not happened. She was going to use this early morning time to gather any sticks that she could find to build a fire.

23

There would be sticks that she hadn't gathered last week as well as others that had fallen recently or that had been blown in by the wind. Using her wheelbarrow, Tina had soon gathered all the sticks that were within close walking distance of the house. The pile of twigs, wood, and sticks was so small this time that she didn't know if it would make a fire big enough fire to heat the water for the laundry.

Thankfully, she had brought a shovel with her as well, which she used to scoop up a couple of dried piles of cow dung. She really didn't like using it because it was stinky, but it would have to do for an outside fire so she'd be able to wash the laundry.

Tina knew the girls would wake up soon and had no time to walk any further to look for more sticks this morning. She certainly didn't want the girls to wake up and become worried when they noticed she wasn't there. Maybe later she would take the girls with her and they could go gather more wood together.

As she neared the house, Tina's thoughts went back to the day before when she had been at her parents' house. She had looked with envy at their large amount of firewood stacked neatly against the side of the barn. What a beautiful sight that had been and how she wished it was hers. *How wonderful it would be,* she thought, *to have all the firewood I needed ready for me.* It was such a simple thing to wish for, but one that was greatly needed at this point in her life. Years later, as she though back to this day, she'd smile and realize it would have been simple enough for her to ask her parents for firewood, knowing how generous they were. But for some reason the thought had never crossed her mind to simply ask, as she and Henry had been so determined to take care of things by themselves.

Laundry day was always a busy day, with the last of the laundry being the worst. There was a bucket in the outhouse where all the dirty diapers were put, waiting there until there were enough to warrant a washing day, which would usually happen twice a week.

During some of the busiest years with babies, Tina would simply hang wet diapers on the wash line outside, leaving them to dry and air out in the hot, summer sun.

Tina carried the pails of soiled diapers out to the large metal wash basin, lifted the lid, picked up the loaded diapers one at a time, dumped out their contents and then tossed them into the water. The smell was terrible! The diapers had been sitting and festering for some days already. Thankfully, it was cooler outside now, so the smell was more manageable than it would be in the hot summer months, when flies and maggots would appear almost overnight.

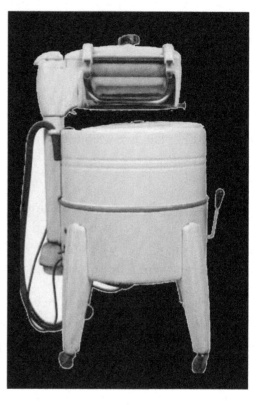

Tina put her bare hands into the water and scrubbed the diapers until they were clean enough to be transferred into the washing machine. In the following years, as the girls grew older they would help her and eventually take over the job of doing laundry and cleaning diapers, but at this stage in time, it was still her job alone.

As she worked, Tina thought back to her teenage years and how she would have used to wash the jeans of the men in her family. Back then, she had thought that those dirty pants had the worst smell ever. The men would wear their pants for a long, long time in between washings. By the time they would get washed, the jeans could often be made to stand up all on their own since they became stiff from the dirt and the milk that would get on them when the cows were milked. The pants would then continue to stiffen as they would get wet then dry again day after day. Tina had thought that the overwhelming smell of old, sour milk was awful until she smelt the dirty diapers that had been sitting out in the hot sun for days.

When the washing was complete, it was a whole other job to clean her hands. It was a good thing that they had strong, homemade lye soap. The powerful soap took care of any smell, but at the same time it left her hands raw and sore if she used it too often.

During those busy child rearing days, the family went on a trip to Canada with a few babies in diapers. There were three children under the age of three with only two of them in diapers. Most of their children were fully potty trained by the time they were two.

There was no extra money for disposable diapers, not even for the occasional trip. In fact, at this stage in their life, a lot of the diapers used were rags and other available fabric. As the diapers got dirty, they were put into a bag and sealed, without removing any of the contents of the diapers. All of it just went into the bag, until there was enough to stop and do laundry. At home, things would have been done differently, but Tina had heard about a newer invention that was becoming more popular: the automatic washing machine. Apparently, there were places in the United States where one could go and do laundry. Someone had told Tina that these machines were so amazing that they could easily wash your dirty diapers for you. If the diapers had poop in them, you didn't even need to shake them out, just throw the whole thing in the washer and all would be taken care of. This was so exciting! It was amazing that such a machine existed, and Tina was eager to try one.

The bags were full by now, so Henry pulled up to the front of a shop where the words "Laundry Mat" were written over the front door. Henry and Tina took the bags of laundry, specifically the diapers, and then instructed the children to stay close to the truck while they walked inside.

Eager to try these new machines, they quickly read the directions and loaded them up and stood there expectantly awaiting the sparkling, clean results that they had heard about. That's when they noticed a problem with one of the machines. It sounded funny and when they peeked inside they saw that it was not draining the water as it should. It was hard to ignore the smell that was coming out of that machine as well, it was filling the whole place with a terrible stench. It was, after all, the machine with all the dirty diapers in it.

"Tina, come here, quick. I don't think this is working like it should." There was a sound of desperation and nervousness in Henry's voice as he called to her.

Tina ran over to stand beside Henry and together they opened the machine, looked at each other, and without a word knew what they needed to do. Henry held the bag as Tina frantically pulled the dripping diapers out of the machine and dropped them into the bag. In that moment, it became very clear to them that throwing fully loaded diapers into a washer was not the correct way to do things. The inside of the machine was evenly and fully coated with poop! That's why the water had not been able to drain.

Frantically, they gathered the rest of their clothes. It did not matter that they were not dry yet, all that mattered at that moment was getting out of that place before anyone else showed up.

"Henry, get the children. I'll finish up here," Tina whispered to him. By the time Tina got outside, Henry had gathered the children and they were all waiting in the truck. Tina hopped in and glanced over at Henry with a smile of relief. Nobody had showed up and their secret was safe, even from the children.

Years later, Tina often wished she could go back and apologize to the owner for the terrible mess that they left in his business. That was not how they normally did things, but that day, shock and embarrassment took over and the only reasonable response they could think of was to run and leave the mess behind.

3 BEING A MOM

It was a Saturday evening; the table was set, and Tina had prepared a simple meal of pancakes topped with vanilla pudding. The pudding was made using milk but was heavily watered down. Times were tight and the little money, food, and supplies they had needed to last as long as possible. Replicating meals and substituting ingredients was a skill that Tina had perfected over time but wasn't as nutritional for her family as she'd hoped.

At school or at a friend's house, the children would see the food other people ate, only to come home and tell their mom about it. It was difficult for Tina to hear her children talk so longingly about foods they would also like to have when she knew that her family simply could not afford it. She wished she could provide her kids with healthier options, but quite often real fruit pies would be substituted with a Kool-Aid pie, chocolate pudding would be made with water instead of milk, and stews would be thinned out to become soup.

Tonight, it was just her and her five girls at home, like it had been all week. Henry was not at home and once again Tina didn't know when he would be back from his trip delivering farm equipment to the States. For him to find a phone to give her a call on the way was not an easy task and Tina never knew how long she would be alone before her husband would be back.

"Girls!" Tina called up to them as she walked to the foot of the stairs. "It's time to come eat!"

Immediately the sound of little footsteps could be heard scampering across the floor and hopping down the steps. The girls knew better than to make their mother wait or call them a second time. The girls were hungry and quickly sat down on the long bench behind the rough wooden table.

"Who's turn is it to share this time?" Crystal asked, looking around at her sisters and then down at the four empty plates on the table. "I've been sharing all week!" she declared. "I really think I get my own plate today, right mom?" She turned and smiled at her mother.

Tina could never remember all the details of who had to share and who could have their own plate, so she turned to the little note pad that lay on the table beside her plate.

"Yes, Crystal, it says that you and Ruth can have your own plates for supper." She patted Crystal on the shoulder then turned to the younger girls.

"Tara, you share with Rose. Bethany and I will share." Tina stooped down and picked up Bethany, who was almost a year old by now.

"Now, let's be quiet to pray." With her free hand she held on to Rose's hand, who was having a hard time holding still. Simply managing to have a moment of quiet to thank God for the food was a struggle.

"Close your eyes girls and nicely fold your hands," she instructed before praying.

Their simple supper was a quick ordeal, almost as quick as

their prayer had been. As soon as the girls were done eating, they left the table and ran back upstairs to play. Tina looked down at the nearly empty table before her and realized there was one good thing about having only a few dishes. The cleanup would be quick and easy, and by now Tina was tired. It had been a long, lonely week. The youngest girls had been fussier than usual due to unrelenting teething pain. As a result, Tina had stayed home most of the week, which did not help her loneliness. Her husband had been gone for six days already and she still had no idea when he would be back.

Slowly, Tina walked over to the old, wooden rocking chair in the corner of the kitchen. She had pushed it up nice and close to the wood stove which currently still emanated warmth from the fire she had made earlier that afternoon. Sitting down, she prayed for a brief moment that the girls would be quiet and content for a while so that she would be able sit for a bit and rest her aching back and legs. She pulled the wooden foot stool closer for her to rest her legs on before she closed her eyes and leaned back adjusting the pillow behind her. It felt so good to sit down and take the weight off her weary legs. But the moment was short lived; a minute after she settled into her chair, Bethany, who had stayed downstairs, came over and asked to sit with her.

"Sure honey, come sit with me." Tina lovingly placed her hand on the little girl's head. It didn't matter how tired Tina was, she enjoyed holding her little children so long as they would sit calmly and not wriggle around.

"Just let me close the curtain first."

Tina gently eased her way out of the chair and walked over to the window. Outside the sun was starting to set behind the distant mountains and Tina did not want to worry about what could be going on out there. Every evening, like clockwork, Tina would make her rounds in the house, closing the curtains and locking the doors. She did this to help put her mind at ease concerning the thieves and robbers that they had been hearing about. She had spotted a couple of horses and riders up on the distant hills beyond their farm late one evening last week. She was certain that those men were not from their colony and seeing them had left her with a knot in her stomach and fearful feeling in her heart.

"Come here, sweetie. Come sit with me."

Tina reached for a blanket and gingerly sat back down once again, adjusting the pillow for her back and pulling up the foot stool. The young child needed no extra coaxing. She clambered up on her mama's lap and snuggled in the blanket. Bethany was happy now, as she was most of the time when she was getting attention, but she couldn't seem to hold still and with Tina's rapidly expanding belly, due to baby number six, she really needed her to hold still.

"How about I sing some songs to you?" Tina asked. "Would you like that?"

She didn't need a response; she knew what Bethany would say. All her children loved it when she would sing for them.

Bethany eagerly nodded her head, so Tina quietly started to sing. Singing helped the girls calm down but tonight it was equally helpful for Tina. It helped calm her down as well, easing the tight feeling of fear in her stomach.

It seemed that every night found Tina afraid. Even at the best of times, a shroud of worry covered her. It would often happen when it was just her and her little girls in the house, while Henry was on the road. She felt so alone, so helpless, in the face of her anxiety. Often, she wondered what she would do if a stranger with ill will showed up on her doorstep. Would she try to ignore them, or would she answer the door? Most often she though that she would try to give her father a call. She was so thankful that her parents lived just down the road from them. She knew that her father or a brother would always be there for her if she needed them.

Some evenings, like this one, the memories of the past were almost impossible to get out of her mind. It was at times like these, when she closed her eyes, she could so clearly remember the events that had taken place at her parents' house only a few years back.

It had been early evening and Tina had been getting the girls ready for bed when there was a loud, urgent knocking on the door. She rushed to see who it might be.

"What's going on?" Tina asked as she opened the door. One of her brothers was standing on her front step, concern written all over his face.

"We just had some thieves break in at our parents' house again," he said, with a shaky voice. "Mom knew you're home without Henry, so she asked me to come let you know about what happened and ask if you would like to come spend the night with us."

"Yes, of course I'd like to come," Tina replied. She immediately started gathering a few things to bring with her.

"Is everyone okay?" she asked, turning back toward her brother.

"I think everyone will be okay," her brother replied, "but Ivan did get shot."

"Shot!" Tina gasped. "I thought you said everyone was okay?!"

"The bullet just grazed the top of his ear, so yes, he will be okay."

By then, Tina had gathered her three little girls and was ready to head over to her parents' house. "Was anyone else hurt?"

"No, just Ivan," her brother replied. "But the man who shot him also walked up to him and, for no reason, just hit him over the head with the butt of his gun."

Tina could tell by his voice that he was worried.

"I don't think he will need to go to the doctor, but he will have a terrible headache for a while. The robbers wanted money of course and after they realized that all they were getting was the food that dad offered them they waved their guns around in anger. We don't think they were intending to shoot anyone, but obviously, they really wanted to scare us."

Now, years later, as Tina sat there, holding her daughter, and singing songs, those unpleasant memories ran through her head. She decided right then and there that tomorrow after church, they would go straight to her parents' house and spend the day there. This decision brought a smile to her face and a lighter feeling to her heart.

It made for a relaxing atmosphere and Tina was soon able to let the stressful thoughts go as she rocked her little girl.

This evening was bath time. The oldest girls cheerfully helped carry water into the house from the tap located just outside the front door. Tina was thankful to have running water on their property, but that didn't mean that bath day was much easier. The water ran so slowly it could take hours to simply fill up the tub as there was very little water pressure. Once inside, Tina heated the water up on the stove. The girls were able to have a nice, warm bath in the large, round, metal tub that sat on the concrete floor in front of the cozy fire.

After that Tina had to get their hair combed in preparation for Sunday. She found that to make Sunday mornings run a little smoother she had to wash, comb, and braid everyone's hair on

Saturday evening.

"Come Crystal, let's try something a little different today." Tina walked over to the table with her comb in hand. She had prepared a bucket of warm water that was sitting close to the table.

"Jump on up here." Tina patted the table and smiled reassuringly as Crystal gave her a confused look.

"You want me on the table, mamma?" Crystal asked.

"Yes, I thought of something, and I'd like to try it tonight. Come, hop up here and then lay down with your head right close to the edge." Tina patted the table, indicating where she wanted Crystal to position her head.

"I'll sit on this chair and that way I can wash your hair in the bucket, and then I can also comb and braid your hair right away as well."

If she could manage to comb and braid all the girls' hair without having to bend over or stretch her back, she would be so grateful.

"Okay, mom," Crystal said. With a little giggle, she climbed up on the chair, laid on the table, and positioned her head close to the edge. Tina had done it so many times that by now braiding her girls' hair only took Tina a couple of minutes. When completed, she tied a kerchief snugly around their heads ensuring their hair would neatly stay in place for church the next day.

"You're done." Tina said as she helped Crystal back down onto her feet. "Please tell Ruth that it's her turn to come down now."

In no time at all, Ruth came down to get her hair done and shortly after, the hair preparation was done. Once done, Tina tucked all the girls in bed upstairs. She then set a small stool in the hallway for herself.

Tina and her 10 oldest daughters dressed up and ready for church.

There was a total of three bedrooms upstairs with Henry and Tina's bedroom being the only one that had an actual door on it. The other two rooms had door frames, but no doors installed. They were small rooms and all close together so Tina could sit and read on her stool, in the middle of the hallway, and be heard by all the children. Occasionally, on special evenings, when Tina wasn't too tired and her schedule allowed it, she would read bedtime stories to the children. Tina did feel very tired tonight, but for some reason, she felt compelled to sit and read to them for a while. Maybe it was because she knew that in a couple of weeks, when the new baby would be born, she would be busier once again.

Oh, what a treat that was for them all! Lying in bed and listening to their mom read a story was simply the very best way to end a day and fall into a peaceful sleep. The girls found their mom's voice to be comforting and relaxing, the kind of voice that made you feel happy and relaxed, for she was the kind of mother that made their young minds believe that all was well with the world.

For Tina, it was a good night as well. As soon as she got into bed, she heard a truck pull into the yard and what a sweet, welcoming sound that was. She knew that Henry was home and her heart immediately felt lighter. In so many ways, it made life much easier to have him at home, and tonight it meant that Tina could relax and finally let the fear of local thieves go. It was also especially relieving tonight because Tina knew that this was the last trip that Henry had planned to make until after their next baby was born.

That evening Tina was convinced that she still had a couple of weeks left before it would be time to give birth to their sixth baby, but no sooner had she and Henry fallen asleep, that she was awakened by a sharp pain and realized she was wrong. She woke Henry up and let him know that she would have to get to the hospital quickly if they wanted to make it there before this baby was born.

Henry jumped up out of bed and quickly rushed to their truck and drove down the road to pick up Tina's brother Ivan. He had agreed to come and stay with their girls if they would need to go to the hospital during the night. In the meantime, while Tina was waiting, she gave Ivan a quick call so he would be ready when Henry got there. In between contractions, she gathered a few things that she wanted to take with her to the hospital. Tina was not accustomed to being this unprepared. Every other time when it got close to having a baby Tina would have a bag packed ahead of time, but tonight she was caught by surprise. She knew that she had either miscalculated the weeks of pregnancy or else she was having this baby too early. For just a moment, she felt concerned about the baby's safety, but her thoughts were soon interrupted by Ivan and Henry quietly walking through the door.

Henry and Tina rushed the couple of miles into town where there was a small hospital, staffed by a couple of nurses along with trainees. The hospital was not equipped for serious medical emergencies nor were they ready to deal with any births that would require medical intervention. The nearest doctor was a couple of hours away and if needed, would come as soon as he could.

Thankfully Tina's babies were all born without incident and today labor took only took a few hours. They soon discovered why the baby was coming early. They were having twins! Totally unexpected and unprepared, Henry and Tina welcomed baby six and seven into their home four weeks early. The newborn twins were so very tiny, only four pounds each, but they were doing well and that gave the parents a lot to be thankful for.

The night was only half passed, and Tina was already resting peacefully in the hospital bed trying to get a few hours of sleep. The nurses were taking such good care of her and doing their best to keep the new babies quiet so that the exhausted mama could get some much-needed rest.

Meanwhile, Henry went back home hoping to get a little sleep as well and allow his brother-in-law Ivan to go back to his home.

Tina and her twins

When Henry walked into their home in the wee hours of the morning he was greeted by a disturbingly sad little scene. A sight so sad that later when he told Tina about it, she struggled for many years to come to peace with what had happened.

There in front of him in the living room was little six-year-old Crystal. She was sitting and holding one of her younger sisters who was crying, a hoarse, quiet cry that was the result of having been going on for a long time already. Henry walked over and knelt before Crystal.

"Where is Uncle Ivan?" he asked her.

Crystal looked up at her father with eyes as round and large as saucers. A lone tear ran quietly down her cheek.

"I don't know," she responded in a whisper. "What do you mean about Uncle Ivan?"

Henry took the little baby from Crystal's trembling hands, carried her around for a few minutes until she fell asleep and went and laid her down in her crib. He came back down to Crystal who by now was shaking and sobbing uncontrollably with her head on her knees and arms wrapped around her legs. Henry stooped down and picked her up.

"I woke up, daddy, and I couldn't find you or mamma." Her voice trembled as she continued. "I woke up because Bethany was crying and crying, and she just would not stop. When I went to find mamma, I couldn't find her, but I saw that Bethany was in her crib. But you and mamma weren't there," she repeated. "I didn't know what to do, so I picked Bethany up and held her on my lap on the rocker."

She lay her head back on her dad's shoulder and her crying subsided.

Henry rubbed her back reassuringly and told her to go back to sleep.

"I won't go anywhere Crystal. Try not to worry."

To his amazement, Crystal did fall asleep in a matter of a few moments and Henry carried her upstairs to her bed.

The next day, upon further investigation, they found out that while Ivan was at Henry and Tina's house, watching their children, someone had broken into his house on the other end of town. Out of fear and desperation, his wife had called him, and he had driven home as fast as he could to make sure that his wife and children were fine. He left thinking that he would certainly be back at Henry and Tina's house before any of the girls there would even notice that he was gone.

Sadly, that is not how it had turned out and that terrifying night experience was the trigger for much fear and anxiety for Crystal. For many years that followed, she couldn't handle being alone and needed to be near her mom for most of her waking hours.

Even up to a year later, as Tina sat in church, she felt a twinge of sadness as Crystal came and squeezed herself between one of her younger sisters and Tina. Her need to be right next to Tina was as strong now as it had been a year ago. Tina knew she must forgive what her brother Ivan had done, leaving her children alone in the middle of the night, that night a year ago. Truly she had forgiven him, he had a good reason for what he had done, but seeing how much it still affected her daughter made it hard.

Tina turned and smiled at her daughter, helping her feel safe and protected next to her.

Perhaps Tina sympathized with her daughter in this regard because of a fearful experience that had taken place earlier that year as well. Unlike Ivan, who had had a good reason for what he did, one of Henry's brothers, Paul, thought it would be fun to play a practical joke on Tina, although it was not well received.

Late one evening, after the children were all in bed, Tina had heard some strange sounds coming from outside the living room window.

"Oh dear, I should have closed the curtains by now," Tina whispered to herself as she tiptoed over to the window.

Reaching over to pull the curtain closed, Tina's knees went weak, and she nearly yelled in terror! There just outside her window stood a man with his head and upper body covered in rags, looking like a mummy!

Oh no! What did he want? Would he force his way into the house? Would he hurt her or the children? Could he be appeased with some food? Tina's mind raced with questions as she stood frozen in fear, unable to bring herself to close the curtain. Then as if in a dream, Tina watched as the man before her slowly started to remove the rags from his face.

"Close the curtain!" Tina's mind yelled at her, but her hand held still. She watched in complete shock and disbelief as the man removed the last bit of rag from his face and revealed the face of Paul, her brother-in-law.

At first glance, Tina could see that there was a mischievous smile on his face that quickly melted into a look of confusion when he saw the effect that his thoughtless and reckless prank had had on her. Tina was finally able to move again and swiftly pulled the curtain closed. Shakily, she sank onto the floor and held her head in her hands. There were no tears as Tina tried to collect herself, and deep down, she knew she had to harden herself against the fear and hardship all around her.

4 IN SICKNESS AND BUSYNESS

Winter had settled in and was making its presence known through the wind that howled around the corners of the small, rustic, one and a half story farm home. The single pane windows continued to shudder and tremble against the unrelenting storm. The sun had set hours earlier, leaving the little home in darkness, save for the single light that glowed softly in the main area of the home.

It was late, much later than Tina liked bedtime to be when she tiptoed over to the corner where the wood stove quietly crackled, emanating some much needed warmth. Very quietly, she added another log to the fire, just for good measure. She was going to bed so late that she had no intention of getting up in the middle of the night to stoke the fire.

Slowly and painfully, Tina dragged her aching body up the stairs to her bed. She was completely and utterly exhausted. It had been an especially long day as she had been looking after her very sick children. Now, at last, they were all peacefully sleeping.

Nearly three weeks earlier, some of the cousins who lived on the other side of town had come down with the measles and Tina's eldest daughters had taken it upon themselves to get sick as well.

They thought that it would be a good idea to get infected and be able to put the illness behind them as soon as possible. It was, after all, something that everyone had to deal with at some point, or at least that's what the girls had heard. They decided that they might as well take matters into their own hands and hurry it along.

Crystal and Ruth decided to set their plan to action and walked down the dusty dirt road to their cousins' house. They may have been a little out of line and on the edge of mischievousness, but their hearts had no ill intent. They never imagined that their actions would make their mother's life very difficult for the next couple of weeks.

Upon reaching the house, the girls went inside for a few minutes to see how the cousins were doing. It became apparent right away by the painful looking rash on their bodies and the puffy, tired-looking eyes that they were indeed very sick. The girls tried to visit for a few minutes, but every time one of the cousins started to say something, they ended up in a fit of coughing that left them unable to speak. The girls quickly decided that it was time to head back home before their mom started to worry about them.

Before turning to leave, Ruth walked over to one of the cousins, reached out her hand, and touched her forehead.

"I did that just to be certain that we would get whatever it is that you have," she explained in a matter-of-fact voice. Sure enough, exactly ten days later the two girls that had gone to see their cousins began coughing and running a fever. They knew at that point that there was no possibility of keeping their little visit with the cousins a secret from their mom.

Timidly, they went to tell her what they had done, hoping that their mother would not be angry with them. Tina listened quietly, in disbelief to their confession.

"You did what?" she asked, as if unable to understand what

they were admitting.

"We are so very sorry mom," the girls said as they hung their heads in shame.

"But we did think it would be a good," Crystal sheepishly tried to explain.

Tina took a few moments to think about what she had just heard. "I suppose it doesn't really change anything," she replied. "It may have happened at another time anyway."

She sent the two sick girls up to their bedroom. The girls didn't realize how much they had to be thankful for that their mother didn't get angry with them. She would have had ample reason to. In fact, any other mom would have been upset. But not their mom. No, she may have shown some displeasure, but anger was not a reaction they received from her.

Tina looked down at the bump that was starting to show from her recent pregnancy. She thought about how this illness would most likely make its way from one child to the next until it had affected all eight children, possibly even the baby. Her mind started racing as she contemplated what the coming weeks would look like.

She was all on her own with eight children, the oldest one only being eight years old, and with a baby on the way. How would she be able to manage things? She had heard a lot of bad stories about the measles and if she let herself dwell on how bad it could be, she was terrified.

Tina did what she always did when things looked dark and impossible. She went to God for help. At this stage in her life, she did not have extended times of Bible study or prayer, as there simply were no opportunities for that. She spent her days with a constant, quiet reliance on God to help her. She prayed and quickly asked God for help and strength to make it through this day and the days ahead.

And so, the days passed and turned into a week, then ten days. Crystal and Ruth had begun to feel a little better over the last three days and were no longer struggling with a high fever or persistent coughing. The remaining children had now begun to show symptoms of the same illness.

Gone were the early, mild symptoms of the virus. They were instead replaced with the acute, serious stage of soaring temperatures, endless coughing, aching bodies, and the appearance of an unmistakable rash that confirmed the disease. All the remaining children, except for the little girl sleeping upstairs in her crib, were very sick. The measles had hit their home with a vengeance!

Tina walked past the only other bedroom that had anyone sleeping in it. She glanced over at Rodi and Sandra sleeping peacefully in the crib they shared. They seemed to be having a peaceful rest. She walked to her bedroom, stooped over the little girl that was sleeping, felt her forehead, and breathed a sigh of relief when it didn't feel hot. She headed over to her bed and laid down without another thought.

Tina was so exhausted that she couldn't remember falling asleep but knew she must have been out as soon as her head hit the pillow. However, as soon as she had fallen asleep, or so it seemed, she was woken up by the worst possible sound, the sound of one of her children throwing up! In a few seconds, she went from sleeping soundly to jumping up and rushing down the stairs to see who was crying, throwing up and calling for her mommy.

There, in the middle of all the bedding, was a little girl bent over, head in her hands, quietly crying. Thankfully, the vomiting sounds had stopped, but Tina knew that the mess was just beginning.

Fortunately, before going to bed last night, Tina had decided to set up a sleeping area downstairs for the sick children. With most of them becoming seriously ill, it made the day run a little smoother if they were able to lie down whenever they wanted to in the main area of the home. This enabled Tina to tend to them while at the same time being able to take care of all her other responsibilities.

After taking care of the mess on the little girls face, Tina helped her change into some clean clothes, gave her a drink of water, and found a clean spot for her to lie back down again. She seemed to be feeling better now and Tina hoped that they would both be able to fall asleep again. She took a moment to look at the other girls and, amazingly, they were all still asleep. She then turned her attention to cleaning up and removing the soiled bedding. She gathered up the blankets that would need to be washed and set them just outside the front door. As soon as the sun was up and she had a few moments, she would go back out and wash them.

Desiring some more much-needed sleep, Tina started to head upstairs again, but before she made it past the first step, there was that dreaded sound again. Tina turned just in time to see another child empty her stomach right onto the blankets they were sleeping on!

Running past the kitchen, Tina quickly snatched a pail from under the sink and hurried over to the girl that was still half asleep but making a terrible mess on more of the blankets. She immediately saw that the damage had already been done and began gathering up the additional dirty blankets. She then proceeded to help her whimpering daughter change into clean clothes and get comfy in bed with a clean blanket.

With all the crying and vomiting, there were no longer any sleeping children. They were all awake and unhappy. Besides the two oldest girls, all the others were looking worse than they had the day before. Tina quickly did what she could to get the five girls that were downstairs as comfortable as possible. She made sure they all got a drink of water and had a warm, clean place to lie down. It was going to be a long day, but hopefully they would all be able to fall asleep again for a little while before it started.

With the contagious nature of the illness, there were not many people that wanted to be around them, making help difficult to find. Tina knew that her mother would have loved to come and help her and would have enjoyed holding the little ones, rocking, and singing songs to them. However, she was needed at home while caring for Tina's sister, Shirley. Shirley was mentally and physically handicapped and needed almost constant care.

Tina knew that although her mother couldn't be there with her, she prayed for her and cared deeply about her. Her mother did what she could by calling and checking up on her frequently. She had also asked a young lady from church to go to Tina's house and give her a hand for a couple of days, which was a lifesaver for Tina.

The sun was starting to come up on a new day, but because of the children's painful eyes and sensitivity to light, the curtains would remain closed for the duration of the daylight hours. Tina missed the warmth and cheer of the sunshine streaming in the front windows, but it was a sacrifice she was happy to make for the comfort of her children. For many days the only light in the house had been a soft glow that came from a lamp in the corner. By now it had been numerous days with such dim lighting and with the prolonged sickness, that Tina was finding the atmosphere to be getting gloomy and sad. To help with this, she found a way to keep the kitchen light on by hanging a paper from the ceiling to keep it from shining into the rest of the house. Even just the extra little bit of light had proven to greatly improve her mood.

Tina glanced over at the girls. They all looked like they were either asleep or getting close to it. Thankfully, with all the activity going on, the three little ones upstairs still hadn't made a sound.

Tina tapped Ruth, one of the older girls, on the shoulder. "I'm going to go out to milk the cow," she said. Ruth gave a faint nod of acknowledgment. "If you hear one of the little ones upstairs crying, please go pick them up."

Again, Ruth nodded and added a soft, "Okay, mom."

"But please keep them quiet as long as you can," Tina instructed.

With a bucket in hand, Tina hurried out the door into the cool, crisp morning. She was in a rush and ran across the yard to the cattle pasture that was beyond. "Come on, come on," she called out, hoping to alert the milk cow to her coming. "Come on," she called again. Thanks to Tina's faithful consistency with offering the cow small treats for coming, the cow was already slowly approaching the gate.

Tina led the cow into the barn. They had done this many times before, so the cow had the routine memorized and walked right up to the manger where Tina gave her some fresh hay to munch on. It had no need to be restrained in any way but would stand patiently as it was milked. Their milk cows were normally gentle and well behaved and this one was no exception. Tina was quite thankful as the milking was most often done by one of her girls. Tina pulled her stool up nice and close to the cow's warm side, leaned her head against the cow's soft belly, and started milking. The cow's warmth soaked through to Tina's shivering body and helped her feel warmer and somewhat comforted. The barn was a calm place to be this early in the morning. All was quiet around them with only the soft sound of the cow chewing her food and the sound of the steady stream of milk being squirted into the metal bucket. Steam rose as the warm milk hit the bottom of the cold bucket.

Today, however, there was no time to linger, no time to enjoy the sounds and smells of the barn. No, there was an urgency in all that Tina did these days. She must try hard to finish the outside chores as quickly as possible and hurry back to the house full of sick children before things got out of hand inside. In recent years, milking the cow was no longer her job. A couple of the older girls would do that as well as take care of the chickens, feeding them and collecting the eggs. In fact, one of the girls had been milking, one of their especially gentle cows, shortly after her sixth birthday. Hopefully, in a day or two, one of the girls would be well enough to get back to doing their outdoor chores once again, taking that off Tina's schedule.

Bucket of fresh, warm milk in hand, Tina put the cow out to pasture again and hurried back to the house. She was so thankful that there was only one cow to milk at this time. Tina thought back to a few years ago when they had up to eight milk cows for a while; that was before any of the girls had been able to help her. Tina always did all the milking on her own, by hand, with no help from any milking machines. She would get up very early, before any of the children were awake, run outside to milk a cow, and run back inside to check on the children. If all was well inside, she would hurry back out and milk the next cow before doing the cycle all over again until she had milked all eight cows. Thankfully, it had not lasted for more than a couple of months as it was simply not possible for Tina to keep it up.

The sounds that greeted Tina when she opened the door and walked back inside were not as peaceful as when she had left. The three youngest girls that had been asleep upstairs when Tina walked out were all up and had been dutifully carried into the main area of the home by Ruth, just as Tina had requested. Baby Lenna, the youngest one, had woken up hungry and was crying at the top of her lungs while one of her older sisters paced the floor, anxiously bouncing her up and down on her hip, desperately trying to calm her down. It was safe to say that no one was sleeping anymore.

Tina reached out and took the baby from her frazzled daughter and, while she cleaned up the milk and eggs with one hand, she held her nursing baby with the other. All the years of having babies while being busy with other children and activities had taught her how to do almost anything while at the same time nursing a baby.

Soon the little girl had been fed and Tina could turn her attention to preparing breakfast for the other children.

"Come girls, come to the table," Tina called to them.

"Mommy, I don't want to eat anything," one of the girls replied.

"I'm scared I will just throw up if I eat anything," another one said, as she laid back down on the blanket on the floor.

"If you can't eat, at least come have some tea or water to drink," Tina said.

She laid the now-contented baby on a blanket and picked up the twins, one on each side of her lap, and fed them some oatmeal. In between spoonfuls for the twins, Tina managed to eat a little as well. Thankfully, the twins both ate well and didn't seem to be running much of a fever yet. It was a good thing that Tina had not made much oatmeal because very little of it was eaten.

After breakfast, diapers were changed and faces washed. Tina took the opportunity to go outside and rinse out the dirty blankets she had set outside earlier. She didn't take the time to thoroughly wash them, that would have to wait until wash day.

Back inside, she busied herself with one child and then another, first rubbing a tummy and then cooling a forehead. Despite there being eight girls, all under the age of nine, with nearly all of them just recovering or dealing with acute symptoms of the measles, it was amazing that the house was as calm as it was. Moving from one child to the next, she checked everyone's fever. Fevers were running high, and rashes were beginning to come out in full. This was the day that all the girls, except for the two oldest and the baby, were feeling the worst. A couple of the girls' fevers were very high, high enough to make Tina concerned, especially for Bethany, the three-year-old little girl.

"You have to lie still, Bethany," Tina instructed. "This cool rag needs to stay on your head, like this," Tina said as she lay the freshly cooled rag on the girl's hot forehead.

"Please help me!" another child cried. "It feels like I will have to throw up again."

"Please use the bucket I put beside you." Tina replied, immediately getting up to give her other daughter a hand. It was too late. The child reached for the bucket but only some of the vomit made it in, the rest went over the edge and onto the floor. Thankfully the blankets stayed clean this time. Cleaning up the mess on the floor was bad enough, but much better than getting more of the blankets dirty.

Before she could finish cleaning up that mess, Bethany, who was crying loudly by this time, had walked over to her with outstretched arms asking to be picked up. Tina stooped down to pick up her little girl and was alarmed at how hot her body felt.

"Oh, Bethany, what will we do with you?" Tina wondered out loud as she held her hand against the little girl's forehead. It felt much too hot.

"Shh, please don't cry sweetie." However, Tina's pleading was only met with louder cries.

She dipped a couple of rags in a bowl of cool water, wrung them out so they wouldn't drip all over the place and gently lay one on Bethany's head. By this time the little girl's cries had turned into screams and had all the other children worried.

"Mommy, what is the matter? Will Bethany be okay?"

someone asked.

"Why is she screaming?" someone else questioned.

"Please make her stop," another said. "It's too loud and it makes my head hurt."

At last Tina was able to get a temperature reading from Bethany despite all the commotion and noise going on around her. Never had any of her children, or anyone else she knew, had such a high fever. It was just over 105 degrees!

Shocked, she sat down in the rocking chair with her screaming, squirming little girl. Bethany was starting to quiet down, so Tina took another damp rag that she had and placed it ever so slowly on Bethany's tummy. This started the screams again, which brought on the coughing, which led to Bethany throwing up and making another mess that would need to be cleaned up at some point.

Fear started to grip Tina's heart. What could she do? Would her child be alright? Should she call someone to come help? In that overwhelming moment when she had no person to turn to, when the day had only just begun and already, she was exhausted, with a floor covered with sick children, Tina turned to her source of strength. Tina prayed. She asked God to heal Bethany, to help her make it through the day and for strength to take care of her children. The days ahead would be impossible without help from her heavenly Father. She poured out her pain and loneliness to God and then she started to sing and soon Bethany started to calm down. Tina kept on singing as she changed the warm rags for new, cooler ones. Tina soon began to feel calmer as well and shortly after that, Bethany closed her eyes and fell into a sweet sleep. Tina then lay Bethany down and changed the rags out for cooler ones again. She felt her forehead and knew it wasn't as hot as before.

By this time, the baby needed to be nursed again and more

diapers needed to be changed. As soon as that task was completed, Tina turned to the table, which still had breakfast dishes on it. She decided to go ahead and serve lunch in those same dishes, as that would save her one small task.

The bucket on the floor was still full from the last vomiting session and should be dealt with before someone else threw up. Tina quickly emptied it out, gave it a rinse, setting it back down where she could easily access it.

So it was that the seemingly endless hours stretched out before Tina turning into days that melted into one another and slowly turned into weeks. All the activities that would normally help pass the time for young children when confined to bed became difficult or impossible to do. The girls' eyes were so sore from the illness that the lights were kept low, and activities like reading, looking at books, or even coloring pages lasted for only a few moments at a time. The children played with toys for a few moments here and there and ended up sleeping a lot, which was great for helping them feel better sooner.

Again, it was the power of God at work in her that made it possible for Tina to make it through the long days and dark nights. There was very little time to think as Tina was kept busy, and she knew that she could not stop. She could not feel sorry for herself, she had to keep going. After all, she had many little eyes watching her and she had to stay strong for them.

In those years of having young children, Tina learned how to die to herself daily in a very real way. The tasks before her were often nearly impossible and never ending, it seemed. Very often she was left alone to face the daily struggles of taking care of a large, young family and their farm. In a culture that gave very little thought to people's feelings and emotions, Tina learned quickly to bury her feelings deep down inside. She found it was much easier to focus on what lay before her in the external world than the often-painful fears

53

and emotions inside of her.

Tina had herself been very sick recently as well. It happened shortly after she learned she was pregnant. At first, she thought it was simply due to her new pregnancy. However, she kept getting sicker instead of better and then the miscarriage happened. She quickly realized there was more going on than she thought. Her stomach was in terrible pain, her head ached, she had diarrhea and, one evening, her fever soared. It didn't matter how many cool baths or how much medication she took, it wouldn't go down. It became clear that she needed medical help.

Tina's brother Mark, the one who had a reputation for his fast driving, was called to help. He quickly got Tina, along with Henry and Tina's mom, to the hospital in a nearby town.

Henry carried his barely conscious wife from the truck into the hospital and laid her on a bed inside. Stepping back from the bed, he noticed a large clump of her hair had fallen from her head and stayed on his shoulder. In silence, he stood at the foot of the bed and watched the doctors and nurses frantically working on his wife. She did not look good and was no longer responding to his questions. The medical staff ignored his questions as they focused on helping Tina who was barely hanging on while he stood at the foot of the bed and started to weep.

The next few hours were very tense and difficult as no one seemed to be certain which direction Tina was going in. Was she getting better or worse? What was wrong with her? It was hard to tell. Then slowly things started to change and late that evening, the doctor gave them better reports. Hope of her recovery was once again coming back.

Late that evening, Tina's fever stayed at a more reasonable place, and she was able to start communicating again. It had been a very long and tiring day and soon the doctor asked them to leave so

Tina could get some rest.

Henry and his mother-in-law walked out to the truck where Mark was waiting for them. They discussed what their options were for the night. Henry didn't have money for a hotel and besides, he wanted to stay as close to his wife as he possibly could. So, the three of them just ended up sleeping outside, right in the open box of the truck.

Morning came, and along with it, the news Tina was feeling better. In only a couple of days, they were all on their way back home again. It was obvious to them that God had performed a miracle and had healed Tina.

5 MOVING AGAIN AND AGAIN

Corruption was running deep in Mexico, finding its way into the remote, Mennonite colonies more and more. Theft, torture, and murder were becoming increasingly common. Simply finding a police officer or government official who wouldn't take a bribe to cover some shady deal or hide a crime had become nearly impossible. It was so bad, in fact, that some families were contemplating moving out of the area.

Many Mennonites no longer felt safe in their community. Thieves had stopped waiting for the cover of darkness to commit their crimes. They were becoming increasingly arrogant and ruthless, brazenly attacking during the day. This also meant more people were getting hurt.

Just this past week Henry's brother Corny had had a robbery at his business during daylight hours. A couple of men had come into his store and stole what they could easily gather. Corny had offered no resistance; however, they still injured him by slamming the barrel of a gun over his head.

After being treated at the hospital for his injuries, Corny had gone back home to where his distraught family was eagerly waiting for him. Henry and Tina had hurried over as soon as they had heard. Word of the attack had spread quickly in town and many family members were already there, to show their care and concern for the young family.

It was a somber gathering. What they had witnessed and heard that day had opened their eyes to how brutal the thieves were becoming. The families knew that since they would not fight back or sufficiently defend themselves, they were much more vulnerable to attacks.

Corny lay on the couch, quietly holding his wife's hand. She sat on a chair beside him resting her hand on his shoulder. His head was bandaged and one of his eyes nearly swollen shut. Obviously still in a lot of pain, he tried not to move and had both eyes closed most of the time. The perimeter of the room was lined with hard wooden chairs or stools, most filled with concerned family member.

Everyone spoke in hushed tones which was contributing to the feelings of fear and uncertainty they all felt. Many questions ran through their minds. What would the future hold for them? Who would be attacked next? The truth was that nobody felt safe anymore. So far, it was mostly business owners who were targeted for their wealth. But they wondered how long it would stay that way before other families were targeted.

Corny and his wife both felt the same: they could not stay in Mexico any longer. They were willing to leave everything behind if that's what they needed to do to get away from the endless fear and danger they were living in. They started to discuss their plans of moving to Canada and no one tried to change their minds. Plans were immediately put in place to sell their house and business to help them leave the country.

Their business had been the third property in their little Mennonite colony to be attacked over the past couple of months that had included bodily harm. The Mennonites did not fight against the thieves because of their conviction to adhere to non-resistance; however, they would always report the incidents to the Mexican authorities. Finally, their reports were taken seriously as the amount of people reporting increased. Within only a few short days, the military showed up with three army trucks full of soldiers. They were looking for a man by the name of Martínez, the alleged leader of the local drug gang. The local people watched in wonder and amazement as the military trucks drove slowly up and down the length of the colony's road. Everyone was on high alert for the next couple of days, eagerly waiting to hear what was happening and if Martínez had been found.

They didn't have long to wait before the story of Martínez 's capture and death was rumored throughout the area. The unofficial story was that the soldiers had found him hiding in his cabin in the wilderness. Unwilling to leave the cabin and come out, Martínez had stayed inside, forcing the soldiers to take more drastic measures. A makeshift tin can bomb was made and one unlucky man had to climb onto the roof and drop it down the chimney. Soon afterward, a very unhappy Martínez came staggering out of the door amidst a cloud of smoke. He was quickly captured, tied up, and thrown into the back of a truck.

The truck with the prisoner headed out of the little village and soon the other remaining military trucks followed. Nobody heard exactly what happened, but it was widely rumored that Martínez never made it to the city he was heading to. Many said he had met a slow and tortured death in a remote canyon somewhere along the way.

The news of what had apparently happened to the local drug leader caused Henry and Tina to wonder if perhaps their recent decision to move to Canada was the still the right choice. Maybe things would be better now, and they would be able to live in peace without constant danger looming over them.

Henry gave it some thought but decided that they would still stick with their plans to move. So, in the summer of 1968, Henry and Tina packed up their family and headed to Canada. They spent only a couple weeks in Ontario before they headed back to Mexico with six of their children. They still had crops that needed to be harvested and it made more sense for them to head back and take care of them than to hire someone else to do the work for them.

The trip back to Mexico was made in a regular cab pickup truck with no box cover on the back. The hours were long and difficult in a space that was much too small for them. With six children plus Henry and Tina crammed into the cab, there was always at least one or two children on her lap. Very often there would be another one curled up and sleeping at her feet. Seat belts were not commonly used at that time and vehicles were often filled way beyond comfort or safety levels. After making sure the driver side door was locked, they would get one of the older children to sit between Henry and the door.

There came a time on the drive that Tina began to feel claustrophobic and didn't know if she could endure the tight space and restless children any longer. In desperation, she asked Henry to pull over and let her ride in the box of the truck. It wasn't at all comfortable! Speeding along the interstate in the back of the truck was windy and cold and Tina shivered as she wrapped a sweater around her body.

There was no proper place to sit or lie down, but as she spent some time trying to lie down between some boxes, it did give her a chance to be alone out in the fresh air. This brief time alone helped her carry on without taking her frustrations out on her children. Time after time, even in seemingly impossible circumstances, Tina, with the strength God gave her, kept her emotions under control and treated the children with patience, kindness, and grace.

Their time in Mexico was brief and very busy. As soon as the harvesting was complete, they drove back up to Canada. This initial move to Canada was short lived and after a couple of months they headed back down to Mexico. They had spent most of the summer months in Ontario, but when it came time for the children to go to school in the fall, they began to think that maybe they should be back in Mexico.

Before they had moved, they had been led to believe that there would be a Christian school started in Stratton, the town they had moved to in Ontario. But there were delays and the school plans had not worked out. The only other option was to send the children to public school as there were no other Christian schools nearby and they had never even heard of homeschooling at this point. Public school was not what they wanted for their children and so, after a couple of weeks, Henry and Tina decided that it just wasn't the right thing for them to do. Their children were just too precious to be sent to schools where the Bible wasn't the foundation of the education, even if it meant moving back to Mexico.

The following years in Mexico were indeed more peaceful. Henry went back to driving a truck in between his farming and mechanical jobs. Tina continued to raise the family along with farming, sewing, baking, cleaning, gardening, and whatever else needed doing. On occasion, she could even be seen out on the village roads helping Henry grade the roads. Tina would drive a tractor that would pull the grater which was being driven and controlled by Henry. Most times when Henry would be working on the roads, he would find a brother or someone from the colony to help him. At times when no one could be found to help him, Tina would leave one of the older children in charge of the younger ones while she would go help her husband.

Truthfully, she did not enjoy doing this kind of work. She found it to be very stressful, but it did give her a little change from being at home with the little ones. At other times, Tina would help Henry out in the shop with his mechanical jobs. Henry would fix any issues that came up in their vehicles and farm machinery as well as doing mechanical jobs for others. While he would do the heavy lifting, she would reach in and do things that her smaller hands were better suited for.

One day during the harvest season, Tina accompanied Henry on a ride to the fields that were located sixty miles from their home, on the other side of a small mountain range. Their threshing machine was there and had been used to do some work for the local Mexicans. When the time came to go home that evening, circumstances were such that Tina was forced to drive a ten speed, manual transmission, loaded truck over the sketchy mountain roads. Never having done anything like this, Tina was completely overwhelmed at the task that was before her. With her heart in her throat and a constant prayer on her lips, she slowly and steadily did what needed to be done and drove the truck safely out of the mountains and back to their home.

That's the kind of lady Tina was. Whatever difficult task she was faced with, no matter how hard it was, she did all she could. She was brave and strong, and, as a result, fear and doubt were defeated time and time again. Even though Henry and Tina did a lot of hard work as a couple, it was still very challenging, nearly impossible, to get ahead financially. As a family, they always had enough to eat, and no one ever had to go to bed on an empty stomach, although it wasn't always very nutritious food. Meat was very scarce in their home, but they had a lot of bread and potatoes, always enough to fill up on. They also had a garden full of other vegetables and, if the summer wasn't too dry, the crops were wonderful and helped their family as well. However, despite the lean years and tough times, Tina was always hospitable. She learned quickly that meals could be stretched amazingly far by adding more water to soup and filling up on fresh buns and butter.

During those years, Henry and Tina had heard that some families were heading up to Ontario to work in the vegetable fields during the summer. Apparently, the fields were very large and the opportunities for work were plentiful. They had heard that anyone who applied themselves well and was willing to do hard work could do quite well for themselves. So, Henry made the decision that the whole family would cram into their truck and head up to Canada for the summer. The trip between Mexico and Canada was made in a short-box pickup truck with a camper on the back. Most of the children would ride in the back, which also held the clothes, blankets, and dishes they took with them.

The first year that they made the trip to work in Southern Ontario was in 1971 and it was quite an eventful experience. Upon arriving in Alymer, Ontario, they were greeted by their employers, who showed them where they would live. Their living space was inside of someone else's house. The home itself was large but their portion of it was tiny; the enclosed porch area would be their home for the summer. Henry and Tina had brought their ten oldest children along and found it nearly impossible to properly fit into the space. They had left the youngest two with family back at home in Mexico.

Tina missed her little ones so much! The baby was only eight months old, and Tina decided they would never leave their little children for that long again. The family that had kept the two children for the summer enjoyed having them over and quickly grew to love them like their own children. While this was wonderful, it also ended up making it very hard for them to let the children go back to their parents at the end of the summer.

Throughout the summer, most of the family worked on the fields from early morning and into the evening hours. During this time, Tina did the cooking, laundry, and caring for the youngest children. After a couple of days, she become very weary of sharing the living space with another family and longed to have a private place for her own family. There was no place for her to be alone with her children.

While Tina had good children, they still needed to have some room to play, and she could not possibly keep them out of the other family's area of the home all the time. On sunny days, it was a little better since they could go outside, but when it rained, there was no way to escape the crowded home. Eventually, Tina mentioned to the lady of the home that she was so desperate to have her own space that she would even be happy with a dove infested barn or hay loft to live in. Having a large, young family truly made sharing a home with another family a very stressful experience. After Tina had expressed her feelings, it took only a couple of days for their employer to find a car garage for them to live in.

The move that evening was quick. With very little furniture and no beds for any of them to sleep on, there wasn't much to move. They had several blankets to lay on and cover themselves with. As for furniture, they had makeshift, empty hampers from the fields, which were used as chairs or benches. Cardboard boxes served as dressers to keep their clothes in. The garage itself was not properly sealed, so gigantic, black, hairy spiders shared the living space with them. They were often seen scurrying this way and that when the lights would go on. But at least it was a place of their own, and for that, Tina was thankful.

After a summer of hard work, the family headed back home to Mexico. The money that they were able to save that first year was used to buy better, nutritious food. They had more meat to eat than ever before, which was so good for their growing family. Henry had also purchased a truck box in Ontario which he used to convert their pickup truck into a long box truck over the coming winter months. It wasn't much, but it did give them a little more space while traveling in subsequent years.

Truck that the family used to travel

The following two summers they did it all over again and brought along all the children, thirteen one year and fourteen the next. Those years of driving up and down to Canada to work were some of the busiest in Tina's life. Every summer, she had a baby to take care of as well as being pregnant with the next one. No stops were ever made at restaurants or hotels. Food was packed for the trip and nights were spent at rest areas along the way. When food would run out, they would stop and purchase more at grocery stores. One of the family's favorite mealtimes was when they would take time to stop at rest areas. They would eat bologna and grape jam sandwiches, drink orange punch, and eat cinnamon rolls for dessert. On rare occasions, they would take the chance to stop and eat when they would see playgrounds and let the children play for a while.

Unfortunately, on one such play stop, their son, Frankie, broke his arm while playing on the slide. As a result, Henry and Tina spent the rest of the day at the hospital with him, while the other children stayed at the playground. Thankfully, they were traveling with some other family members who were able to stay and watch the children until they got back.

At night, anyone who could fit in the truck would consider themselves lucky to be able to sleep with a roof over their heads. The others would take a blanket and sleep outside on the grass, making sure to stay in the lighted areas underneath the rest area lights. The next morning, before they would leave, head counts were always made to ensure no one was left behind.

The second and third years did provide them with somewhat better living conditions than the first year had. They made their home inside a barn located on a working farm. Most of the barn was still being used for the animals so the smell of manure hung rich and heavy in the humid summer air. There was no air conditioning, fans, or windows to open, so the heat was often overwhelming. The floor was made of rough concrete that had two gutters running the full length of the barn. The back portion of the barn had been converted into basic living area by erecting some plywood walls. The inside of the gutters had not been cleaned out and were filled with old manure that would need to be removed before anything else could be done. It was only slightly better than living in the barn alongside the animals, but at least it was a place of their own. Tina's kitchen was very primitive with very little to work with. She started out the summer with only a hot plate for cooking then halfway through that harvest season, she was at last able to use a stove.

Some days, all Tina could accomplish was taking care of the youngest children since it was a full-time job. She was also the one who did most of the other tasks that would come up, such as grocery shopping, doing laundry in town, and running other errands. On top of this, she would occasionally work in the fields, alongside her family, picking tomatoes and cucumbers. Tina was often so tired from her busy days and the lack of sleep, due to having young children as well as an itch that kept her up for hours every night. She resorted to laying on her stomach out in the field and slowly inching her way along while she picked the vegetables.

It was amazing how hard the family would work. The long day's work made for sore, aching backs at the end of the day and, despite the heavy load that Tina already carried, she would often take some medicinal rubbing alcohol and lovingly give back rubs to her children before they headed off to bed. The children always knew that their mom would take as good care of them as she could.

The family filling hampers with field vegetables

At other times when motivation was getting a little low among the children, Henry would set goals for them and give rewards when those goals were met. Swimming at a nearby pond was a wonderful reward at the end of a particularly hot, humid day and, occasionally, eating store-bought cake with ice cream was a real treat as well. A nearby town had weekly auction sales which the family started going to occasionally on Saturdays. These outings became a highlight for the whole family.

It was nice to get out and do something fun and entertaining after a long week's work. They also took a trip to Niagara Falls and to local zoos as rewards for all the hard work they did. Tina always remembered the first time that they tried French fries and donuts.

They had never heard of these things before! What delicious food! The donuts that they tried inspired Tina and her daughters to try their hands at making some of their own years later. The donuts they made turned out to be so good that they became a sought-after treat in the local area.

The remainder of the year, when it wasn't harvesting time, the family would be back in Mexico. One of those winters, Tina's mom wasn't feeling so well. Slowly over the months, her health declined more and more, leaving those around her worried about whether or not she would ever get better. Then late one Saturday evening Tina heard the phone ring. She quickly rushed to pick it up.

"Hello?"

The voice on the other end of the line was quiet and weak. "Tina, it's your mom here. Would you want to come over and spend some time with me tonight?" She paused for a moment, then softly continued. "Come lay down in bed with me and visit a little. Would you do that?"

"Of course, mom. I'll be right over."

This was not a usual request from her mom and it left Tina feeling sad and concerned. She quickly gave the older children instructions on what to do and told the younger ones to make sure they were good and listened to their older siblings. She then rushed over to her parents' house.

Opening the door, she was greeted by her father who looked very tired and serious. He let her in and then went to sit quietly on the couch while Tina walked over to her mother's bedside.

"Hi mom, I came as quickly as I could." She leaned over and kissed her mom on the check and softly stroked her forehead.

Her mother looked up at her, gave her a weak smile, and gently patted the spot beside her. Tina walked around the bed and laid down beside her mom.

"I love you mom." Tina's throat ached as she tried to keep the tears from falling. She reached over and took her mother's hand and tenderly held it in her own as they spent the next hour in sweet companionship, knowing that this may be the last time they would be able to spend time together like this. They also spent time in silence.

Tina always knew that her mother loved her so much. She knew that her mother prayed for her a lot and that it was because of her prayers that she had the strength to carry on when things in her life were too hard for her. Although they didn't often talk about the hardships in her life, Tina knew that her mother understood and cared. Tina was so thankful that her mother had taught her to bring everything to Jesus in prayer and to live a life of trust and dependence on the Lord. The following week, some of the local school children stopped in at her parents' house and sang for her mother one last time.

With deep sadness and grief, Tina watched as her mother's health deteriorated more and more, and in March of 1972, she left this earth to go be with her heavenly Father. Tina was thirty-seven when her mother passed away.

Petkaus' last house in Mexico

Considering how many children Henry and Tina had it was a bit surprising how rarely one of them had to be taken to the hospital for either sickness or injury. One of the worst incidents was the day that Kenny, their youngest son, overdosed on Benadryl pills. Tina thought that her little son was peacefully sleeping in the crib, but when she started hearing strange sounds come from the bedroom, she quickly went to check. Shocked, she saw an open bottle of pills spilled all over the crib and floor.

"Oh, no!" she gasped. How many of these pills had Kenny taken?

She reached for her son who was whimpering and seemed to be very unsteady on his feet. Instantly, when she picked him up, she felt that his body was warm to the touch and just did not feel right. When she tried to set him on the floor, his legs buckled, and he would have crumpled to the floor if she had not caught him.

Not knowing what else to do, Tina hurried to the phone and called her brother Mark, asking him to come over right away. He was the one who was always called upon when someone needed to get somewhere very quickly. Sure enough, in a matter of a couple minutes, he had arrived and they were on their way to the nearby town. While she had been waiting for Mark to arrive, she had called the little clinic in their village. The nurses there had advised her to head into town as they were not equipped to help her son.

They drove as quickly as the bumpy roads and truck would allow. Kenny cried at first, then start moaning and throwing up while writhing in pain. The little boy was in great turmoil. His little body convulsed, and Tina could feel his heart racing. Soon after, his body became rigid and he was not able to sit anymore.

The road went down through a small creek and Tina asked her brother to stop the vehicle and let her get out for a moment. She carried Kenny down to the water's edge, hoping that somehow cooling his face would bring him a little relief. It did not and in her heart, Tina found herself releasing her little boy to Jesus. She could hardly bear to see the pain he was in. She wanted God to take him out of his agony, so she asked God to take him home.

Amazingly, God choose to spare Kenny's life and, over a short period of time, he was healed completely.

When spring came in 1974, Henry and Tina decided not to go to work on the fields in Southern Ontario. They would make the move back to Northern Ontario instead. Their biggest reason for not staying in the Northern Ontario area back in 1968 was the lack of private Christian schools. But now, a couple of years later, one had been started in a little town called Stratton. So, with their fourteen children and a six month pregnant Tina, they made the long move up to Stratton, the little town where Tina would spend the rest of her years.

Upon arriving in Stratton, the home they moved into was a temporary one. It was a tiny little structure right in the middle of the small, rural village of approximately one hundred people. The home had no hot water and no indoor toilet, but that was nothing new as they were used to the same conditions in Mexico. The main floor of the house served as the living area and kitchen, while the upstairs had a couple little bedrooms.

It was easy to put three children in each of the beds as there was no room for more beds. Thankfully, it was summer, so there was no need for the children to spend much time in the house.

The search for a farm property began right away and later that year they moved into their own home a mile out of town. For the first time, Tina experienced what it was like having hot running water and an indoor toilet. It was also the only other home that she would ever live in. When they moved in, the home was quite small but within a couple of years, an addition greatly increased the main living area and gave them more bedrooms and an extra bathroom. The property was also large enough to allow Tina to continue farming, which she enjoyed very much. There were large areas of pasture for cattle as well as barns for chickens.

Petkau Family Farm in Stratton

The family was finally settled in their own home and the following year was the last summer that some of them made the trip to Southern Ontario for work. After that, life became more settled in Stratton, and they were able to let go of those long trips and summer field work.

6 WALKING THROUGH THE SHADOW

At first, Tina didn't think much of it. Her itchy skin bothered her mostly at night, and not even every night. It was just an annoyance most days. Her life was busy, her days were full, and she was taking care of their four very young children. On top of that, Tina's tummy was getting a little bigger every day. She was pregnant with their fifth child; all within five years.

One day, while Tina and her children were at her parents' house, she mentioned her frustration to her mom. Neither of them had ever heard of someone dealing with this issue before, and after some discussion, they decided it must be due to the dry skin Tina had. She spoke to no one else about it and waited quietly for things to change. Her mom prayed for her and would occasionally ask her how things were going, caring about her like only a mother could. In the difficult and trying years that followed, Tina knew that her mother was fervently praying for her, and there were times when it seemed to be the only thing that kept her going.

A couple months later, on a cold October night, Bethany was born. It was a tradition in their village for a young lady from church to go help the new mothers for a couple weeks after having a baby. Tina was thankful to have help with the household chores so she could try to rest as much as possible for the next six weeks.

Her strength and energy were slowly coming back when a realization hit her: her skin was no longer itchy! She could lay still in bed and rest without needing to constantly scratch herself. It was so relieving to have her skin calm down. It felt so much better!

But alas, the relief was short lived. Three short months later, she became pregnant again, with twins, and soon after realizing she was pregnant, the itch was back! And that is how it continued for the next nine years and seven pregnancies. Every time, shortly after becoming pregnant, the itch would come back to torment her. Then, a few weeks after the babies would be born, the itch would subside. It was somewhat like contractions during labor, only on a much larger scale. There would be months of intense itch that would then be graciously followed by a short period of relief. Oh, the short months of relief were so sweet, but it made the turmoil of the months of itch seem more and more intense.

The year 1973 brought with it one of the hardest summers that Tina had ever experienced. It started out well, with the birth of their precious little baby girl, Danielle, their fourteenth child being born at the end of May. It was in the days and weeks that followed that Tina waited expectantly for her skin to calm down. However, the future started to look much more difficult.

This time after her pregnancy, things were different. Tina found no relief. No break was given to her from the relentless itch. Her skin kept crawling and could not and would not stop! Confusion set in. What could be different this time? Would this terrible affliction really never stop? Slowly, the months passed and turned into a year. Her heart sank and hope had all but faded away as the reality of what was happening became clearer. She would be stuck with this itch, probably, for the rest of her life.

In the years that followed, Henry and Tina welcomed two more little girls into their home. After each birth, Tina was hoping and cautiously expecting that the itch would leave as it had in the past. Tina had felt like she could manage the itch during the pregnancies, if it meant she could have a couple months without it. She had come to expect that the itch would always be there during pregnancies, that maybe even the pregnancies caused the itch. As difficult and hard as that may have been, Tina knew that surely the children that God had blessed them with were always worth the trial she had to endure. It made the struggle more tolerable.

But this time, it wouldn't stop. The months passed, turned into years, and still, it didn't stop. The future looked bleak with no end to this nightmare in sight. Tina felt like a prisoner in her own body, never able to escape the painfully annoying, relentless itch.

"God, I need help!" was her constant cry. "I need healing and deliverance from this affliction. More than anything else, I need hope and rest."

It seemed to her as though God was silent. At times, she wondered if He heard her at all. Surely God could heal her, so why didn't He? Tina pleaded with God daily for her healing, as did her husband and children. At times, she grew impatient and discouraged at the silence.

It seemed neither help nor answers could be found, but as confusing and frustrating as it was, Tina never got angry with God. She bore the burden well. She knew that during the struggle and trial God was with her. Even though it made no sense, Tina knew that God loved her. She never doubted that. She trusted that He was using this pain to make her into a better person and that God would use her and all she went through to bring glory to His name.

Over the years, many doctors were visited and just as many remedies were tried. Tina was desperate for help, so when she was directed here and there by well-meaning people, she would most often try the ideas and treatments they suggested. There were also people who gave her ideas and remedies to try that were not good.

Often, they were simply thoughtless or quick responses that didn't mean much, but Tina tried most anything just in case something might help. It was no use; nothing made the itch go away or subside.

Some suggestions and opinions people shared with her were just plain painful and rude.

"If you would just stop imagining that you have an itch, you would realize that it is just in your mind."

Or "If you would just stop scratching, then the itching would stop," as though the act of scratching made her itch flare up.

A disturbing memory for the whole family was the day that Tina decided to give raw, ground liver a try. The atmosphere in the home that day was somber and quiet. Everyone could see the partially liquefied, vile-looking liver through the clear containers that sat on the counter. Tina would never draw attention to herself and the difficulties she had. She didn't ever complain, but this day, everyone knew she was doing a very difficult thing.

This was a very hard thing for Tina to do. She drank the disgusting liver slop every day for a while. There was no complaining or feeling sorry for herself, only the strong resolve to try anything to make the horrible itch go away. Of course, neither the liver nor any of the other supposed remedies did any good, but that is how it continued. People would come up with more and more remedies and Tina would try them.

While this was going on, Tina maintained a full and busy life. She and Henry had sixteen children, a large garden to grow their own food, and a farm that gave them milk, eggs, and meat. On top of that, Henry was gone most of the time, working as a truck driver, leaving Tina to take care of most things at home on her own.

The exhaustion for her was real and consuming. Many evenings when all the children were finally in bed and the house was quiet, Tina longingly thought back to the days when the itch would leave in between her pregnancies. Those had been the nights when, at the end of a long day, she would go to bed and, before she was entirely in bed, she would already be asleep. Sadly, those nights were a thing of the past, replaced instead with endless, sleepless nights of tossing and turning, trying to find a few moments of peace for her body. All too often those nights left her more exhausted than rested.

A fact that nobody seemed to understand was that nights were always much worse than the daytime was. If she was moving around, she felt much more able to deal with the restlessness and discomfort. It was when she would lie down and be still that the itch became all that she could focus on. Lotions, creams, and ointments of every variety were tried, but no real help was found with only a couple moments of relief here and there. Tina found that if she kept herself cool, almost uncomfortably so, the itch was a little more manageable. In her creativity and innovation, Tina made a blanket for her and Henry that was thick and fluffy on one side while thin and cool on the other side. However, quite often, she could not stay in bed and hold still. She had to get up. She had to move around to maintain her sanity.

It was in the wee hours of the night, as her family slept peacefully around her, that she would tiptoe toward the light that shone under the bathroom door. One lonely wooden chair awaited her predictable arrival. There, in the quiet of the night, she busied herself with embroidery, knitting or some other similar craft. She was lovingly creating small masterpieces of art for her children.

Some of Tina's pillowcases

She would not waste those sleepless night hours with worry and stress. Instead, during those heart-wrenching, difficult hours, a mighty prayer warrior was born! Those were the nights that drove her to her knees, like nothing else could. As a result of those hours of prayer, lives were changed, hearts were softened, and miracles happened.

Tina talked to God about everything. She told him all that was on her mind. The foremost thought on her mind was always the children, that they would always love God, follow him with all their hearts, and love each other as well. In those years of deep trial and struggle, the foundation of a strong, intimate friendship with Jesus was growing. But no time of prayer would be complete without a time of thanking and praising him. She knew that therein lay the strength that she needed to keep going.

Tina was also determined early on in her life to not allow any hardships to go to waste. She knew that God always had a purpose for everything, especially the hard things. Verses that went through her mind a lot were 2 Corinthians 1:3-5, *"Blessed be the God and Father of our Lord Jesus Christ, the Father of mercies and God of all comfort, who comforts us in all our affliction, so that we may be able to comfort those who are in any affliction, with the comfort with which we ourselves are comforted by God. For as we share abundantly in Christ's sufferings, so through Christ we share abundantly in comfort too."* Tina firmly believed that the trials she went through and the comfort she received from God were meant to help her comfort others and understand their trials better.

Hopefully by the time morning came, Tina would have gotten her average of three or four hours of sleep. That was the amount of sleep she got for many, many years. In fact, years later when the itch was gone and Tina could sleep better, she would say that she felt like something was missing if she wasn't up for at least an hour or two to pray at night.

But for now, as Tina emerged from her bedroom in the morning, no one would have ever known what her night had been like. She always emerged from her bedroom with a smile, a real smile that came from her heart and lit up her eyes. A smile that was there because she was living proof that the command to, *"Rejoice always, pray without ceasing, give thanks in all circumstances,"* was possible, and was being lived out. As the children slowly came out of their bedrooms and into the kitchen for breakfast, every one of them was greeted with a smile and a cheery "Good morning." None of them ever heard their mom complain!

Tina kept her struggles very much to herself. In retrospect, years later, she thought maybe she should have talked about them a bit more. Even her husband and grown children didn't truly grasp how difficult things had been. There were, however, a couple times when one of the children saw tears running down her face, even as she tried to hide them by looking the other way.

One such occasion happened on a trip that Henry and Tina took to see family down in Mexico. Trips like that were normally made quickly, only stopping when necessary. This time, they had taken a detour through California to do some sightseeing along the way. The trip was especially difficult for Tina. She felt like she should be having a good time; after all, everyone else was. But her heart was sad. She was tired and finding it difficult to keep her customary smile on her face. As they drove along on the scenic Californian coastal highway, Tina looked at the beauty outside, but inside, her heart was aching. If only she could find relief. She was so tired. If only things were easier... Tears rolled down her cheeks as she turned to look outside, so that the child beside her wouldn't notice.

Moments later, Henry pulled over beside the road to let everyone get out, stretch their legs, and take a break from the drive. They had stopped at a roadside area with beach access. Tina got out, turned to help the children out, and strangely, felt her heart getting lighter. They walked down to the beach and Tina felt unexpected joy and energy in her step. It took a few moments for her to realize why she felt so much better. She was not having any itch!

Just like that, with no apparent reason, she was free of all the discomfort and pain of the itch that plagued her day and night. She stopped in her tracks, turned her face up to the sun and simply basked in the wonder of it all. What a miraculous sensation! Her skin was calm, comfortable, and her body had peace, complete peace. Walking on the beach that day was something Tina never forgot. It was a miracle. It was a kindness from God, and Tina knew once again, more confidently than ever, that He was with her and always cared about her. The next morning the itch was back, but Tina's faith had been strengthened, and she knew that she had been touched by God himself, even if only for a day.

Setting aside time for prayer and fasting was also a discipline that Tina made a habit of doing. Her fasts would often last for a day or two at a time. She would still make delicious meals for her family and continue to go about her daily work schedule as she normally did. Her children would observe this and would, from time to time, join her in her times of prayer and fasting. One day, the whole family decided to fast and earnestly pray for Tina's healing. Everyone could participate if they wanted to, but no one was forced to. Tina felt so honored that her whole family would do this for her that at the end of the day she made a large scrumptious dinner and dessert to thank and bless her husband and children.

Unrelated to the itch, Tina also noticed that she had some lighter spots on her skin. Over time, this became a lot more noticeable, and it began to bother her a lot. They lived in a very sheltered community at that time, with little interaction with the outside world, so nobody knew what this skin issue might be. No one else had it and Tina very often felt embarrassed. It was only years later, after moving back to Canada, that they found out it was a common skin condition called, vitiligo. Knowing that it was not an illness was relieving, but the stares and judgment from ignorant people over the years had left their mark on her self-image and confidence.

Along with the itch, came a whole new set of skin issues, sores, and infections. Even before she bent down to look, Tina knew by the moisture on her fingers that she had, once again, scratched her leg so hard that she had made herself bleed. The few moments of relief it gave her, made it seem almost worth it. Oftentimes she was just so itchy that she simply could not stop herself; she would scratch so vigorously that the bleeding would start. Eventually, she had sores all over her body that often became very painful. They would get infected and would cause pain and more itch, and the cycle would keep on going.

The doctors didn't know how to help her. Biopsies and other tests were done over and over, but no answers were ever provided. Then came another possible remedy. One of Tina's sisters and a sister-in-law had heard about a man in the United States that claimed that the right vitamins and minerals could heal almost anything. So, with their help, a lot of tests were completed, and it was determined that, among many other lesser deficiencies, the biggest problem for Tina was that she was suffering from a damaging lack of calcium.

A treatment plan was very carefully prepared on the premise that vitamins and minerals were supposed to help her, that this would be the cure that she had spent years looking for. At the onset of the treatment, Tina was told that it would not be a quick fix, but rather, it would very likely take a long time before any difference was even felt. Tina had battled with this itch for twenty-seven years, so she was told that it could take up to twenty-seven months of faithfully taking the vitamins and minerals before she would feel better. This, however, did not discourage Tina. The plan made sense, it sounded reasonable, and she was ready for the long journey ahead. If she could be feeling better in 2 years, she was willing to give this treatment a try.

Much research had to be done into what type of vitamins and minerals would be the best quality, while still fitting in their budget. So many years had passed with no help, they were willing to pay almost anything while looking for a possible solution for Tina.

At last, a lot of pills were purchased, and the experiment was about to begin! Tina got up early the very next morning, like she always did, and counted out her pills for the day, sixty in total, plus some additional liquid vitamins and minerals. She also made a large pitcher of lemon water that she placed on the counter. She then set a timer to remind herself to drink half a cup every thirty minutes throughout the day.

This schedule kept going for the next month or so and, suddenly, the day came Tina was looking for. One morning, when

Tina got up she thought she may have fallen asleep a little better than the evening before, but, on the other hand, it couldn't be true. It had only been five weeks since the beginning of the treatment plan. Surely there wouldn't be any noticeable difference yet. So, she stayed quiet and didn't mention anything to anyone else yet. What if it was just wishful thinking on her part? But then, when week six came, she knew things were changing and she started letting herself feel hope again. She started to think that she might be getting healed after all.

Two weeks later, at only two months, not twenty-seven months as she had been told, Tina knew for sure that the treatment was indeed working. For the first time in years, she could relax when she sat down in the evening, she could fall asleep faster, and her sores were starting to heal quicker than new ones were forming! Tina's heart sang and in her joy she echoed the same words that Mary, the mother of Jesus, said so many years ago, *"My soul magnifies the Lord, and my spirit rejoices in God my Savior, for he has looked on the humble estate of his servant... He truly has done great things for me, and holy is his name!"*

From my perspective:

As a little girl my bedroom was just down the hallway from my parents' bedroom, and I would always go to bed to the sound of my mom scratching. I almost feel bad, but for me, it was somewhat of a comforting sound. It let me know that my mom was close by and, in my little girl mind, she was perfect. She didn't need much sleep. After all, she was always awake when I was, and she was always happy and thankful.

I always prayed for her before going to bed. But I never really understood how difficult it must have been for her.

It sounds crazy when I say it, but I never heard my mom complain about her itch, literally never. Nobody did, because she just didn't complain. She was strong, stronger than anyone else I've ever known. She had such a deep resolve to always do the right thing and to live her life in obedience and submission to God. Never in all these years of struggle did she feel angry with God or question his love for her. My mom's faith was firmly anchored in Christ; it never once wavered.

How could my mom endure all those years of hardship with the intense itch that she had?

I asked her that question just a little while ago and, after careful thought, she said, "I think it was the prayers of my mom that did it. I always knew that my mom loved and cared for me and that she prayed for me to be strong and to endure whatever difficulties I would face in life."

As I sit here and ponder that, I think of my mom's prayers, how they have carried me, and still do even when she is no longer here. When I miss her, I remind myself that her legacy of prayer lives on and will for many generations to come.

7 TRAIN TRACK ADVENTURES

Tina quietly made her way into the living room, tea in one hand and her Bible in the other. It was still early and the only other people up were a couple of the older girls who were preparing their lunches and hurriedly eating breakfast before heading off to work. She sat down and before opening her Bible she simply reflected on life for a while.

Life was a lot different here in Canada than it had been in Mexico. In Mexico, they had lived in a small Mennonite colony and seldom left its safety and familiarity. They knew everyone that lived nearby, and they all went to the same church while the children attended the same school. Life was predictable with very few surprises as well as very little influence from the outside world. In many ways, that had been a much easier and more relaxing lifestyle.

Things were not the same here in Canada. They no longer lived in a Mennonite community. In fact, there were very few Mennonites living near them. Tina felt concerned. They no longer had the support and safety net of a large group of people that lived the same way they did, believed the same things, dressed in similar ways, and spoke the same language.

Here they were not like most people around them. Tina and her family were used to speaking a dialect of the German language, Low German, while most others spoke English or High

German. Her family still dressed in conservative Mennonite clothes and the women wore head coverings after they were baptized. No one else did that in their new place except for a handful of people. There was a little church in Stratton that they attended for many years where a wide range of backgrounds were represented. Some had lived in Canada for many years, others were recent immigrants from Switzerland, and the few Mennonites who attended ranged from more liberal to quite conservative. Of the more traditional group, the Petkau family was the most conservative.

Tina was alright with that. She believed that they were living their lives as they believed they should, but she just looked at it differently now that they didn't have the support of many like-minded people around them. Now, they would have to learn to stand on their own. They would need to be okay to not lean on other people as much. They would have to be fully convinced of what they were doing and have good reasons for why they were doing it.

She may have been able to get away with it before, but now, she knew that she would not be able to tell the children to do things simply because that is how they have always done things. She would need to have good reasons. Tina knew that now, more than ever before, she would need to know what the Bible said. She would need to have Biblical answers for the children. When they would ask her why they were expected to live, act, and dress in a certain way, Tina always gave the best answers she could, very often with her Bible in hand.

The family farm was located adjacent to a busy railway track. Hearing the blaring horn ring across the fields, every fifteen minutes, as it passed the crossing less than a quarter of a mile down the road, was very common during the day, with less frequent crossings at night. The family learned to block out the sound of the train, even becoming oblivious to the rattling of the dishes in the glass hutch in the kitchen. Visitors to the Petkau farm did not have the same experience. They were often jolted awake in the middle of the night by the blast of the train horn. At other times, they were not able to sleep for most of the night. To those not used to the effects of the train, the rattling of dishes in the kitchen cupboards was often thought to be the sign of an earthquake.

Much entertainment was had with the train tracks over the years. Many times, they would take walks along the tracks as they ran through beautiful woods and fields. Those who were feeling adventurous would attempt walking on the narrow tracks, testing their balance. No visit to the Petkau farm was complete without a souvenir: a flattened penny. Coins would be carefully placed on the tracks just before the train crossed. Then, as soon as the train was gone, they would race back to the tracks and search for the flattened coins in the rocks nearby.

Train track that ran past the Petkau farm

The pasture for their cattle went right up to the track. On occasion, Tina had gotten a phone call from the train conductor

himself, letting her know that a couple of their cows had been
spotted out of the fenced area and were in the ditches beside the
track. Those were always embarrassing calls to take, yet she was so
thankful that they would care enough to notify them.

Perhaps the most memorable experience involving the
train was when Tina joined a couple of her daughters outside with
some farming tasks one day. Henry and Tina owned several fields
and pastures on the other side of the tracks and, today, Tina had
asked her daughter Bethany to take the tractor and disc to work on
the opposite side of the tracks.

Tina busied herself in the garden and paid no attention
to Bethany as she left the yard and headed toward the field. Only a
few minutes had passed when Tina noticed strange sounds coming
from the tractor. She looked up from what she was doing and walked
towards the dirt road to get a better look at what was happening. She
wondered if the tractor was stopped on the tracks. She couldn't tell
for sure, but it did appear that way. Not sure what to think, Tina,
slowly, started walking toward the tracks. A moment later, Bethany
jumped off the tractor and hurried around to look at the equipment
attached to the back of it. She bent down and looked underneath it,
as if there must be a problem. Tina started walking faster. Surely
stopping right in the middle of the tracks was not a good idea.

In the next moment, Bethany was back on the tractor,
aggressively revving the engine, but it did not move. Black smoke
rose from the muffler as Bethany tried to get the tractor to move
forward, then backward, but to no avail. At this point, Tina was no
longer walking. She was running! Her daughter was indeed stuck on
the tracks, and in the distance, a couple of crossings away, they heard
the dreaded sound of a train horn as it was approaching.

"Mom! I'm stuck!" Bethany yelled as Tina approached.
"What are we going to do?"

Tina had reached the tracks and could see that the disc was stuck on one of the railway planks that was sticking up, slightly, from last winter's frost. One of the tines appeared to be firmly stuck in the wood and wasn't about to budge without a serious fight.

Then it came again, the blast of the train horn as it was now a mile closer.

"Keep trying to move the tractor!" Tina instructed. "We have to get this thing to move!"

Frantically, Bethany tried to jerk the tractor forward, backward, then forward again. She turned to look at Tina, fear in her eyes as in the distance they could see the smoke rising from the approaching train, and she realized she was not having any success.

"Bethany!" Tina yelled above the sound of the tractor. "I will run towards the train and try to warn them to stop."

Bethany nodded.

"You keep trying to move the tractor off of the tracks," Tina continued. "But if the train gets past those trees right there and you are still stuck on the tracks, you jump off and run to safety." Tina instructed. "Promise me, you will jump off in time, so that you won't get hurt!"

Tina looked her square in the face until Bethany gave a solid nod, "Yes."

And then, Tina ran! She ran like she had never run before and, as she ran, she took off her hat and waved it wildly in the air. The train driver couldn't hear her but that didn't stop her from yelling.

"Stop! Stop!" she cried as she ran right toward the train that was steadily approaching, slowing down a little because of the slight incline before her.

There was a loud screeching of brakes and billows of black smoke as the train driver noticed Tina and quickly applied the brakes, doing his utmost to stop the train. But a loaded freight train was not an easy machine to stop. The train was at least a mile long and required a long time to come to a halt, but not today. All of its braking power would be put to the test. Tina jumped off the tracks and into the tall grass growing alongside the tracks as the train, brakes locked in place, rumbled past, still going much too fast. All that was left for her to do was pray, and that is what she did. Frantically and desperately, she prayed the train would stop in time.

No sooner had Tina jumped aside for the train to pass than she was running again. This time, she was running alongside the train and yelling for her daughter, who was still on the tractor, to abandon it and run to safety.

"Bethany! Get off that tractor!" Tina yelled.

There was no way Bethany could hear her, but Tina kept running and yelling. The train would not be able to stop. It was carrying far too much weight and had far too much momentum.

Why was Bethany still on the tractor? Could she not see what was about to happen? Panic set in and fueled Tina's weary legs as she kept running. The tractor was moving only slightly, rocking back and forth with all of Bethany's efforts.

"Bethany!" Tina yelled.

And then, in what seemed like the last second, the tractor lurched and backed away from the tracks. The train, still moving at a considerable rate of speed, disengaged its brakes and kept on going.

Tina stopped running. The train was now between herself and her daughter, who was on the other side of the train. She bent over, gasping for air. Her lungs screamed in pain as she tried to catch her breath. That had been much to close for comfort. What if the tractor hadn't moved? Would her daughter have made it off the tracks or would she have stayed, trying her best to move the machinery? Her mind spun with thoughts and unanswered questions.

On the other side of the tracks, Bethany sat in shock, her white-knuckled hands still clutching the steering wheel of the tractor. Her heart was in her throat as she contemplated the past few minutes. She knew she had stayed on the tractor too long. What if it hadn't moved? Would she have made it off in time? She also knew that on the other side of the train, her mother was most likely asking herself the same questions.

Thankfully, the incident from a few years earlier had had a different outcome than this one. The Petkau family was moving a small house, from town, onto their yard. It would serve as a place for grandparents, cousins, newly married children, sisters, or brothers to live in, whenever it was needed.

The crisis on that day had been very similar to this one. As the house was being moved over the tracks, it had gotten stuck, and, just like today, the sound of an approaching train concerned everyone. A small crowd had gathered. They were desperately trying to move the house, while a couple of the girls took off running toward the train as fast as they could. They were going to warn the train driver of the situation ahead, hoping that he would be able to stop the train before it reached the crossing. They were afraid that the house would not be moved off the tracks soon enough.

Brakes had locked, wheels had screeched loudly in protest, and smoke had billowed. The train had not been loaded and the girls had had a head start, so on that day, the train had been able to come to a full stop about a hundred feet from the crossing where the house was stuck.

"Looks like you're having some trouble up ahead," the conductor called to the girls through the open door of the train.

The girls were bent over trying to catch their breath.

"Thank you so much for stopping!" one of them was finally able to call out. She walked up to the steps of the train. "We are moving a house and it got stuck on the tracks."

"I can see that," he responded. "It's a good thing the train wasn't loaded. If it had been, there is no way on earth that I could have stopped in time." He motioned for them to come closer. "You girls look tired. Why don't you hop up on here and I'll give you a ride to the crossing?"

That brought a smile to their faces, and they quickly jumped onto the steps of the train car. That was a pretty special gesture as neither of the girls had ever been inside of a train before.

"Thank you so much," they both exclaimed. What a nice treat to be offered a ride in the train of the man that they had just inconvenienced.

Once they were aboard, the train started to slowly inch forward never going faster than a couple miles an hour. After a couple minutes of crawling down the tracks, it once again came to a stop a couple of feet from where the house was stuck.

Many apologies were made and, after a few more minutes of feverishly working, the tracks were cleared, and the conductor and his train were free to be on their way.

By this time Tina no longer had young children and found she had more time to teach her girls how to cook meals and bake bread, pies, and cookies. On days when they made homemade noodles or perogies, they would set aside all day for that task. They would make extra to freeze, hoping to have enough for at least a half or a whole year. Pies were also done in this way. In the summer, when the fresh fruit was available, Tina would make blueberry, rhubarb, strawberry, raspberry, and other fruit pies to last the year.

Most of the time, there would be three large freezers full of food in their basement. They were farmers and grew most of what they needed to eat. Every year, the family would butcher their own beef, chicken, and pork. They rarely needed to run to the store for things such as fruit, vegetables, meat, eggs, milk, or cream. Sugar, flour, spices, and some fresh produce in the winter months was all that came from the grocery store.

During the winter months, Tina would do a lot of sewing. She had taught all her girls how to sew their own dresses as well as many other items. She also made sure that each one of them sewed and quilted a large quilt of their own. This became somewhat of a rite of passage into adulthood.

Another hobby that gave expression to Tina's creativity was liquid embroidery. Tina would put patterns onto blocks of fabric. She would then stretch them out over embroidery hoops until the fabric was nice and taut. Then, she would paint the pictures with little tubes of paint, shading and blending the colors, creating beautifully colored paintings using fabric as her canvas. The completed squares would then be sewn together and quilted into beautiful blankets or pillowcases. One of Tina's biggest embroidery projects was a blanket with birds and flowers that she painted with her liquid embroidery and then brought to the Sewing Circle ladies at church to quilt. This blanket was sold off at an auction sale in their small town.

Quilt Tina made for auction sale

One beautiful summer day, the whole family headed to Manitoba. It was time to take a mini vacation together and they had decided that the Mennonite Heritage Museum in Manitoba would be a great place to go. What a fun day it was, looking around and learning more about their heritage. Games were played and souvenirs were purchased. The best part of the day was when Tina was given a special gift from the Museum. They honored her with a small gift because she was the woman who had come to tour the museum with the most children. Tina did not like to be the center of attention, but she had to admit that it had been special to be recognized.

Another year, they loaded up a couple vehicles and took a trip to Thunder Bay and Kenora. They stopped at a couple of attractions and spent the night in a hotel before heading back home.

Over the years, they made many little trips like this. They became known as Family Outings. Years later, as the family became larger, trips of this nature became too difficult to coordinate. The family then decided to switch over to have family gatherings at camps in Ontario, Manitoba, or Oklahoma. Tina always really enjoyed these times of being together. Seeing all the children and grandchildren, having time to visit with them, and hearing them sing and tell stories of their lives brought much joy to her heart. She especially enjoyed the singing. That was always the best part of any time together. Tina could never get enough of the music, it brought her so much joy.

Tina loved the old hymns, especially those that spoke of heaven. As the years went by and the children left home Henry and Tina discovered and enjoyed a newfound hobby of playing harmonicas together. At first, they only played at home when they were alone. When they mastered the skill, they enjoyed playing for their family, friends, church events, and at retirement homes, bringing smiles to countless faces.

8 WEEKENDS IN THE EIGHTIES

Saturdays in the eighties were wonderful! They would consist of days spent with family as most of the children would be home for the weekend. Tina would get up before everyone else to have her devotions in the living room. This way, she would be ready to chat with the children as they would take their time by slowly coming down for breakfast.

On Saturday mornings, Tina allowed the children to sleep in and have a relaxing start to their day, but 9:00 a.m. was the cut off time for breakfast. If anyone hadn't eaten by then, they would have to go without. Tina knew they were still most likely sneaking food after that, but she was okay with that. At least she could clean up the breakfast dishes and get on with the day.

Saturday mornings were spent cleaning the house and doing jobs around the yard. Everyone had a job, from the youngest to the oldest. Most days there was a lot to do, and the children worked hard. At other times, when there was not so much to do, everyone took advantage of the slower pace. The older ones would take a lot of time to visit while doing their jobs and the younger siblings did a lot of playing. The three brothers would work on the trucks, making sure to fix any problems that had come up over the week. They also made sure to find and prevent any problems that might come up in the next few days.

Tina enjoyed those mornings, seeing all the children happily doing their jobs. There was rarely any grumbling among the children and the love and joy among them made her feel happy. Oh, she was thankful when the children cheerfully worked together while enjoying each other's company and completing the tasks they needed to do!

In the house, the younger girls would be dusting or doing some other menial tasks and, as they worked, the radio would be playing loudly in the living room. A local Christian radio station played children's stories and songs every Saturday morning, called, the *Children's Bible Hour* and the girls looked forward to listening to it all week along. Tina glanced over at them and was amazed at how it was possible to take so long to wipe just a couple pieces of furniture. But it was okay. They were occupied and doing their jobs well.

One Saturday morning during summertime Tina had asked a couple of the girls to go work outside in the barn.

"Hurry up, Rodi!"

It was a beautiful Saturday morning and Sandra wanted to get work out of the way before noon. On Saturday afternoons, they could have free time if the work for the day was completed by then. Quickly stuffing the last bit of breakfast into her mouth, Rodi followed Sandra out to the barn.

The barn was big, red, and old, the kind that existed on every large farm back in those days. The inside was dimly lit, smelling of musty hay and cow manure even though the pens were now empty. These were mostly used in the spring for calves that needed extra attention or for cows that had had a hard time giving birth. Now that spring was over and the cattle were all moved back outside, it was time to clean out the dirty stalls.

The twins were happy they had gotten this job today. They

preferred being outside rather than staying inside to clean the house. They didn't waste any time and got right to work. Once this job was completed, they could spend the rest of the day doing whatever they wanted to do. One of the pens in the barn had a large window inside, which was easily removed and set aside. One of the girls quickly went to get the 4-wheeler, attached the trailer to it, and parked it just outside the barn window. This way, they could simply throw the manure and bedding out the window, unto the trailer, and then haul it away to the pile in the pasture, causing the job to go by much faster.

Tina and daughter

They had just picked up their pitchforks when Tina came walking in. She was in her black rubber boots, still wearing an apron. She came into the barn, picked up a shovel and, with a smile on her face, got right to work alongside her girls. The girls were happy, but not surprised, to have her there.

This was not unusual behavior from Tina. She would often go look for the children that might be having the least desirable job and help them. She loved working alongside her children, teaching them, encouraging them, and simply spending time together. Tina made it very clear to her children that she was never above the jobs and things that they needed to do. She did not hesitate to join right in.

An hour later, when Tina walked back inside, the house was clean, and lunch was already made. After lunch was eaten, the girls cleaned up the dishes while Tina went to have a short nap. She did this regularly because like her mother had told her once, "I know I'm a better mom if I take a little break."

Tina lay down, but that day, rest did not come. Her normally peaceful girls were arguing in the kitchen. She wasn't sure whose fault it was, but she did feel that this was happening too often. Doing dishes should be easy enough, but, for some reason, that seemed to be the time that there were things to fight about. She wondered what it could be this time. Maybe someone was too slow or too fast or too careless. Or maybe the one who was washing dishes had put wet dishes on top of the ones that were partially dry already. But more than likely, it was a heated discussion on whose responsibility it was to dry and put away the tray once dishes were done. Tina had talked to the girls about this so many times, but to no avail.

Praying to God for wisdom, Tina got up and walked over to Jenny and Destiny, who were beginning to wash the dishes. The only thing they had been busy with, until now, was arguing. They both heard her footsteps approaching and the embarrassment was clearly visible on their faces. As unhappy as they were with each other at that moment, no one ever wanted to disturb their mother's nap. Everyone knew how little sleep their mom got at night, and they all treated her afternoon nap as somewhat of a sacred, quiet time. They weren't sorry that they were arguing, but they sure wished they had done it quietly!

"Girls, no more arguing," Tina said in a calm voice.

"Sorry mom for being so loud," Jenny said quietly.

"I'm so sorry we didn't let you sleep, mom," Destiny added.

"I forgive you, girls," Tina responded. "But more important than my nap is that you learn to do the dishes in peace." She walked over to the sink, put her hands in the warm water and continued. "You two go get a chair and sit down and be quiet. You can sit there and think about how you will do better in the future. I will do the dishes."

"Oh no, mom, please let us finish. We can do it very quietly. Let us show you," Destiny pleaded in a quiet voice.

"Yes mom, please go back and have your nap," Jenny said, her voice hardly louder than a whisper.

"Stop, girls. Now, just go and be quiet," Tina responded, remaining steadfast in her decision.

Jenny and Destiny went and sat down, their heads bowed, sitting solemnly, and hearing their mother do the dishes that they should have been doing.

Meanwhile, Tina quietly did the dishes, praying the whole while. She was tired of the constant dish drama. She asked God for wisdom again as she did so many times. She prayed for there to be an end to the need to count how many items each girl had washed or dried, the importance of the water needing to be exactly a certain temperature, or any of the other issues that they could come up with.

When she had completed the task, she walked over to where the girls were waiting on their chairs, gave them a smile, and said they could go now. With peace in her heart that she had done what would teach the girls better than any words would have, Tina went back to her room and decided to still have her nap. She was certain that the house would be quiet for a while now.

Later, when Tina got up, she looked out the window and saw the boys and a couple of the girls enjoying a fun game of baseball on the freshly cut green grass. She stepped out onto the deck and was greeted with cheerful chatter. Her husband, Henry, was still sitting on the garden tractor in the shade of the tall cedar tree in the front yard. He had finished mowing the lawn and was now having a cold Coke. A few of the girls sat on the grass close to the tractor. They were also enjoying a drink and munching on some strawberries from the garden. The work was done for the week and the family was enjoying their typical relaxing Saturday afternoon.

"Mom, would you and dad play a game of croquet with us?" one of the girls asked.

"Sure. If you set it up, I'll join you." Tina responded.

"I'll come and play for a while too," Henry added.

Saturday afternoons went by much too quickly and soon, it was time to make supper. Tina made soup while her daughter Lenna made homemade chocolate cake. Once the soup was simmering on the stove, Tina quickly made some of her simple, yet amazing vanilla icing to top the chocolate cake that they would eat for *faspa* on Sunday.

Then, precisely at 4:50 p.m., the radio was turned on so Henry and any of the children who wanted to, could listen to the show *Unshackled*. Every week, they would hear a different inspiring story about people who had lived in bondage until their hearts, minds, and lives became freed by the saving grace of Jesus Christ.

Tina would seldom sit down to listen to the full story with the rest of the family, but she did hear bits and pieces of it from where she was whether it was the kitchen or some nearby area. It was a good time of day for her to sit and do some knitting or embroidery, providing that all else had been completed. It was very rare for Tina to sit and not do something with her hands. The inactivity always made her itch worse, so she tended to keep herself busy.

Later that evening, there would be board games played on the long kitchen table. Somebody would be boiling potatoes in preparation for Sunday dinner while others would be playing their musical instruments downstairs. Henry and Tina had bought the children a couple of accordions, guitars, and an organ. Tina loved the sound of the music from the children. Oftentimes, she would ask the whole family to get together to sing and play music.

Over the years, it had become a tradition to sing a couple choruses or hymns, right after everyone was done eating, at the supper table. Sometimes, on a relaxing winter evening or weekend they would get the tape recorder out and record some of their songs. Tina loved the singing and music time so much!

Tina playing the organ

The next day was Sunday and Tina was up before anyone else, having her devotions in the living room where she once again saw everyone as they came upstairs. She greeted each of them with a cheerful "Good morning!" and a smile on her face. Breakfast would usually be made by one of the older girls while some good ol' country gospel music was playing loudly from the record player. The music was usually what would wake everyone up, signaling that breakfast was ready.

Being at the breakfast table at exactly 8:30 was very important to Tina. She would not tolerate any tardiness or laziness.

"Quickly now, girls," Tina said to the two girls who came rushing in from doing chores outside. They were cutting it a little close today, causing Tina to wonder if they had stayed in bed too long or if the milk cow had been farther back in the pasture than usual.

Warm tea was waiting on the table and could be enjoyed as soon as anyone sat down, but before eating, Tina liked when the family sang a couple of choruses. She could see that some of the children enjoyed this, while there were others who did it grudgingly, just because they had to. She still believed it was a good thing for the family to do as it helped them to focus on what Sunday meant.

Before heading off to church and Sunday school, dinner preparations were started; this way, there wouldn't be a long waiting period between arriving home from church and dinner time. Punctuality, especially when it affected mealtimes, was very important to Tina.

Everyone, not just the children, went to Sunday school and then stayed for the church service that followed. The Petkau family attended a small Evangelical Mennonite Church in Stratton for many years. Not many activities took place at their small church, but Tina really enjoyed taking part in and leading the monthly sewing circle for numerous years. Sewing blankets for the needy was something that Tina felt was a valuable ministry as well as very enjoyable for her. For many years, her sister Martha and her family also attended the same church, and the sisters would go to sewing circle together. That had been a lot of fun for the two of them!

Sunday afternoons were spent in leisure activities. Sometimes friends came over to visit Henry and Tina and, at other times, the children would either have friends over or would go to a friend's house. Regardless of what everyone was doing, there was always something going on at the Petkau household. Sometimes, walks on the country roads would be enjoyed, occasional baseball games were enjoyed by the whole family, as well as music or games of many varieties.

As Sunday came to an end, preparations for the new week would begin. Downstairs, Tina would sort the laundry into piles, the right size and color, that would make perfect loads for the washer. She would plan to be up early on Monday morning to get a head start on the day.

Outside, two of the older girls were picking some of the

earliest corn that was ready and digging up some new potatoes. This produce from the garden, along with a couple dozen fresh farm eggs, would be going with the boys as they headed out on the semi-trucks that evening. For a couple of years, all three of their sons would leave Sunday evening and return on Friday. Among the three of them, they would drive two trucks. Sunday evenings they would drive part of the way up to Red Lake, which was about a five-hour drive north of home. They would spend the week hauling logs from the forest to the pulp mills, where the logs would be made into paper.

Over time, they had become regular customers at the restaurant of a small truck stop. It didn't take long before a friendship had begun between them and the owner. When he learned where the brothers were from and that he could get fresh produce through them, he began asking for home-grown produce to use in his restaurant. When Tina found out, she was delighted to sell the produce from her garden to be used in a restaurant. She loved having a big garden and being able to sell fresh food as well as make a little extra money.

9 EATING OFF THE LAND

Tina knew how to run her household well, there was no doubt about that. It ran like a well-oiled machine. She and Henry had sixteen children, one of which was married and living a mile down the road.

As the years went by, more of the children found spouses, got married, and started their own families. Others would leave for a couple months or years at a time and then come back. For some, it was teaching at private Christian schools in Texas, Oklahoma, or Manitoba; for others, it meant taking care of one of Tina's sisters in Mexico, who was mentally and physically handicapped. Others went to Bible school, short-term mission trips, or nursing jobs abroad. Tina always encouraged her children to go ahead and do the things they were called to do. Then when it was time to come back home, Tina would always be standing at the entrance of their home waiting for them. If she could make it in time, she would go rushing outside to welcome them back home, with open arms and a big smile on her face.

At home, on the farm, there was always lots to be done, especially during the summer months. Tina always had a very large garden! In fact, many people called it a field and, as the years went by, it grew larger and larger. Then, when there was no more room for expansion, a new garden was made elsewhere on the yard. Sections of grass or a portion of the field would be dug up and converted into a garden.

There were many reasons for keeping such a large garden. The most obvious was that it gave the family healthy, organic produce. Every year, enough vegetables were frozen or canned to last through the winter. Potatoes, carrots, and onions would be stored in a cool, dark, and dry storage area and would often last until next year's crop was ready to be harvested. The health benefits were many, but the money it saved the family was also a big motivator.

Then, there was also the money that could be made from the sale of fruits and vegetables. People from around the county would come to buy the strawberries and raspberries that Tina and her girls would pick for them. Tina was a bit of a perfectionist in some areas, and her garden was no exception. She did not want other people to come pick fruit, carelessly leaving some of the ripe fruit behind to be picked off by birds or left to rot. Instead, she insisted on picking the fruit herself or with her girls. The garden needed to be kept in good condition, and waste was not looked upon lightly.

Tina also knew that keeping people busy often kept them out of trouble and taught them the value of hard work. Those were probably the biggest reasons for the garden being as large as it was. There were, after all, lots of hands to keep busy over the summer months, and Tina took this job very seriously. She worked hard at instilling a great

Tina working in the garden

work ethic into all her children. To her, being a part of the family meant that you had to take part in the work. Truth be told, sometimes Tina would just sit and think of jobs for the children to do, not so much because these tasks needed to be done, but because the children needed to stay busy.

Today, as she looked out over the garden, she noticed something that needed tending to. There was a low, creeping weed that was spreading throughout the whole garden. Every year, they would work all summer to get rid of it, only to have it return even stronger the following spring. She knew that this weed was harmless, and whether they succeeded in getting rid of it really didn't make a difference. It stayed low to the ground and didn't choke out any of the other plants. It was like a short, soft carpet that would never leave and, as she looked across the rows, she had to admit it almost looked nice. Tina walked back inside to where a couple of the girls were finishing up the breakfast dishes.

"Girls, today I want you to work on pulling the *fatie hein* out of the garden."

"Sure thing, mom." Their reply was instant, though the disappointment was easily seen on their faces. They had just made plans to go play outside as soon as they had finished doing dishes, but that would now have to wait.

"Do a good job, and I'll pay you a little for it," Tina told them. "For every pail of weeds that you pull and remove from the garden, I will give you five cents."

"Oh, thank you mom!" Knowing there would be a small payment made the job much easier to do. Money was not often given for jobs that they did, so when it was, even though it was a small amount, it was very special and helped motivate the girls to get things done.

As soon as the dishes were put away, the girls went straight to their job outside. They decided that if they quickly finished the work, there would be more time to play later. This was also one of the things that Tina had tried to teach all her children early on: work first, then have free time later. "If you don't want to work, you shouldn't eat," she would tell them.

At first glance, the weeds in the garden were somewhat overwhelming at this time of year. The five youngest sisters stood and looked over the rows, each one quickly trying to claim the area with the least weeds in it.

"I think we should just go in order from oldest to youngest with choosing a row to weed," Jenny, the oldest one present, suggested.

"What puts you in charge?" Sherry questioned.

"It's easy, I'm the oldest, and that means you all have to listen to me," Jenny replied.

"Okay, let's do that," Danielle said, trying to avoid any further arguments. "I think it's a good idea."

They had figured out a long time ago that it was best if they picked the rows in the garden that they would weed for the rest of that season. That way, if someone didn't do a good job one time and weeds reappeared quickly, they would have to deal with that same area again next time.

"Here are some hampers to put the weeds in."

The girls turned and were surprised to see their brother Kenny standing behind them. This was wonderful, more help to get the job done!

"Mom said that she wants us to remove the weeds from the garden once they are pulled," he said, dropping the green hampers onto the ground. "Kris is on his way with the four-wheeler and trailer. We can dump the weeds into the trailer and bring them into the cow pasture when we're done."

A couple of hours later, they had each made around half a dollar and the job was finally complete.

"Come sit in the shade here," Tina called out to them. "I have some cold peppermint tea ready for you."

Tina made the best peppermint tea in the world, and she knew that it was always a treat for anyone. Having done a couple hours of hard work, Tina was happy to let the children spend time playing in the afternoon. The yard was big, and the children's imaginations were even bigger. There was so much fun for them to have, and they would often disappear for hours at a time. There was an old, abandoned school bus hiding in some brush in a corner of the back yard. Much time was spent in and around it; seats were taken out or moved around and it became a well-loved play place. The big red barn had a large hay loft that was most often full of square bales. The bales could be moved around to make rooms or even tunnels. There was even a time or two when tents would be set up among the bales and nights would be spent in the barn. The purpose of the tents was to keep the mice off them, but for those brave enough, blankets were sometimes laid directly on the bales.

Wild blueberries, Northern Ontario gold, was something that Tina and her family loved finding, picking, eating, and selling. They would often go to great lengths to find the delicious little berries. As the berry picking season would approach, Tina would keep her ears open for any good places to go picking. And every summer, without fail, the Petkau family would find places where the berry picking was good, and they would get to work picking as many as they reasonably could.

"Frankie, when you go up to Ear Falls this week, please ask some people you meet if they think it will be a good blueberry year," Tina said to her son, who would spend all week driving a truck a couple hours north of home.

Sure enough, the next weekend when he got home, Frankie said that it sounded like it would be a good idea to head up that way to pick berries. Tina knew that it would be a long drive and that she would have to plan the event well so that it would be a success. She was very good at planning things, organizing, and making almost anything happen, if given the opportunity to do so. Before long, she had come up with an idea and quickly the rest of the family was on board with making it happen.

Early the next Friday morning, three vehicles packed full of people, food, water, blankets, and pails headed up to the Ear Falls wilderness. It was a four-and-a-half-hour drive to the northern town, but even then, the trip was not over. From there, they followed a bumpy dirt road that was mostly used by the semi-trucks, bush equipment, and other vehicles working in the logging industry. They chose this location to pick blueberries because some of the men working in the bush had said that there were a lot of berries close to their bush camp. Tina held a roughly drawn map in her hands as she navigated.

"I think you should pull over here and let someone go have a quick look," Tina suggested.

Henry pulled the van over to the side of the road. No sooner was it parked, than a couple passengers jumped out and ran onto the large rocks and into the new forest growth. The spot they were at had large rocks that were partially exposed. Most of the trees within a couple acres had been forested about three to four years back. There were some new, young pine trees starting to grow back in between the rocks. It was a beautiful Canadian shield landscape.

"Come!" one of the girls called out excitedly, as she came running toward the van. "It's looking good out there. Come on, come check it out!" She quickly made her way to the back of the van to grab a pail and headed back into the woods.

Tina got out and made sure that everyone had what they needed whether it was pails, water to drink, bug spray, or snacks.

"Do you want to come with us, mom?" asked the girls who had stayed behind with her.

"Sure," Tina replied. Then, with a smile on her face, she walked into the bush beside them.

Tina absolutely loved this! Being out in nature so far away from civilization was so peaceful, so refreshing, and so relaxing. She stopped for a moment, closed her eyes, and just breathed in deeply. The smell of warm summer days in the woods, pine needles and dirt, all mixed with the faint smell of freshly cut wood greeted her. The loggers had completed their jobs here and had moved on, leaving the area quiet. The sound of laughter and talking from her family was the only noise to be heard. She walked over to the edge of the rock that she was on and sat down on the moss-covered dirt and pine cones.

The blueberry picking was exceptionally good. Tina could sit and fill her pail without needing to move around much. She wasn't quite as fast as some of the others who could pick a full gallon in twenty minutes, but that was alright with her. She still managed to pick much more than she had expected.

At the end of a long, productive, blueberry picking day, everyone got back into the vehicles and drove down the road a short way. They stopped close to where there was a large logging camp. It was the one that Henry and Tina's sons worked with and where they had planned to park for the night. They positioned their vehicles in the shape of a triangle, which left space on the inside of the triangle for almost everyone to put a blanket on the ground and sleep under the stars. The stars shone bright that night, far away from any light source. The night air began to cool down, and far in the distance, so far that they knew it wouldn't bother them, was the faint sound of rumbling thunder.

Picnic lunch while picking blueberries

Henry and Tina slept in their car with the seats reclined as far back as possible. Tina looked out of the window and felt such a deep peace and joy in her heart. She knew that they were making wonderful, rich memories. As she looked at the children laying outside, and she listened to them chatting into the late hours of the night, she thanked God for this precious opportunity. She looked up at the moon shining brightly and at the stars twinkling on this clear summer night. The temperature was perfectly comfortable, and the bugs were leaving them alone. It was only in the wee hours of the night when Tina was finally able to fall asleep, but that was alright. It was so good to be here, to rest, and to see the children growing quiet and falling asleep one after another.

Morning came quickly, it seemed. Having just spent the night in a car seat, Tina was surprised that she had slept as much as she had. She looked outside the car window and noticed some of those sleeping on the ground start moving. Wanting to create the most beautiful and cheery morning possible, Tina put a tape into the tape player of the car and quietly opened her door, letting the soft, gospel music flood the area, gently waking the rest of the children. For many of them, waking up that morning was said to have felt like waking up in heaven. It was the sound of the music and the smell of a nearby campfire that coaxed them out of their slumber. There was not one complaint about the sleeping conditions that night. The hard ground and the light sprinkle of rain had not dampened anyone's spirits.

On the drive home that evening, a lot of stops were made. They stopped at gas stations, grocery stores, and a lot of tourist shops to peddle out their gallons of blueberries. Tina was amazed and felt so blessed at all the success they had. Prices were even better than she had hoped and the number of gallons they had sold before getting home was more than anyone had expected.

10 BEING A GRANDMA

Becoming a grandma was one of the best things that ever happened to Tina! It all started one morning in mid-April. The phone rang and Tina hurried over to answer it. She had been on her way outside, but thankfully hadn't left the house yet.

"Mom, this is Garry."

Garry was her oldest son-in-law and receiving a call from him was not unusual. But today, Tina could immediately hear his shaky voice and knew this was no ordinary call.

"Crystal is in labor, and we are heading to the hospital now," Garry said, quickly. He sounded excited and concerned at the same time. "Mom, will you please pray for us?"

"Sure, I will, Garry," Tina replied. "Now, just relax and go help your wife have a baby."

The hours passed slowly that day and Tina could not think of much else other than her eldest daughter was giving birth to her first grandchild. After six hours of hearing nothing, Tina could wait no longer. She left the children at home, asking the older ones to look after the younger ones, and headed off to town.

When Tina arrived at the hospital, she was quickly shown to her laboring daughter's room. The relief on Crystal's face when her mother walked in was easily seen. No one could bring comfort and encouragement to a tired, pained, and worried daughter like Tina could. A couple of hours later, a perfect and precious little baby girl was born and, just like that, Tina became a grandma.

Tina was from a generation that was very hard working and believed work to be quite important, so it may be somewhat surprising that they strongly believed women should take it easy for the first six weeks postpartum.  Women in postpartum recovery were not supposed to sweep or wash the floor. They were encouraged to walk as few stairs as possible and get all the help they could for tasks around the house. The mother's primary focus during those first weeks were to rest and recover, focusing on taking care of their newborn baby.

As often as she could, Tina tried to pass this teaching down to her girls, hoping that they would do the same and give their bodies a chance to fully recover after giving birth.

However, as the years went by and the younger daughters started their families, Tina found it difficult to watch them stop taking it easy for as long as she thought they should. She would tell them if they overdid it physically, they would pay for it later. However, culture around them had changed as well as the traditions surrounding childbirth and recovery.

Whenever any of Henry and Tina's children had a baby, Tina made it a priority to go over to the hospital or their home as soon as she possibly could to give the baby a bath. She was proud of the fact that she was often the one to give the newborns their first baths. For Tina's daughters, it was such a relaxing thing to have their mother come and take care of their babies. It was a chance for them to relax, fully knowing that their newborns were in the best care possible.

Newborn babies were definitely Tina's favorite! She would often be holding a baby if there were any babies around. When her daughters would come visit with fussy or sick babies, Tina would very quickly relieve the mother of the crying baby. She would lay the baby down, rub its tummy or back, wrap it in a blanket, and proceed to sit down and snuggle the child. She would give the babies water with syrup or chamomile tea in a bottle and, all the while, her daughters didn't question her methods. They all had complete trust in their mom. Normally, in no time at all, the previously unhappy child would settle down and become calm and quiet. Their grandma had the most calming, peaceful, and reassuring way about herself, causing the babies to be just as peaceful.

On one occasion, one of her daughters pulled into the driveway, parked her car, and slowly got out. The car seat pulled out of the back seat contained a crying newborn, that could not be calmed down. The exhausted and sleep-deprived daughter made her way into the house and, with tears in her eyes, handed her little, discontented baby boy to her mother.

Tina emanated such sweet, calm confidence as she picked up the baby and, with a smile on her face, started talking in reassuring tones until the baby was quiet.

"Go have a nice warm bath," Tina said, as she gently patted her daughter's shoulder. "Then, lie down and have a nap."

"Are you sure, mom?" she asked, hesitating for a moment.

"Yes, and don't worry about a thing," Tina continued. "I'll come and get you once your little one is hungry."

"Thank you so much, mom," her daughter said. She smiled faintly and walked downstairs.

How blessed she was to be able to come and leave the baby with her mom, even if for only a couple of hours and have some time to rest.

As the grandchildren grew older, Tina loved playing board games with them. She was also getting older and found some activities, that she had previously enjoyed, were now more difficult to do. Board games were one of the things she could easily do with them, and she had taught many of the grandchildren how to play a variety of games with her. She showed three- and four-year-old, wiggly children how to play *Memory* and explained how to play *Dutch Blitz* to some teenage boys. While they played, she would engage them in meaningful conversations.

Years later, when many of the grandchildren were young adults themselves, some of the granddaughters had prepared a special spa evening for Tina along with other aunts and cousins. The downstairs of Henry and Tina's house had been transformed into a lovely sitting area. A fire crackled in the stove, giving off a soft, inviting glow in the otherwise dimly lit room. The flickering light of candles added to the intimate and festive atmosphere.

Holding tightly to the handrail, Tina carefully took the last step down, walked over to the comfiest chair, and took her seat. The chairs were set up in a circle with a comfortable rocking chair for the honored guest, Tina. In front of the chairs, buckets of warm water had been filled with the best essential oils and Epsom salts, garnished with fresh mint leaves that floated on top. In the center of the room sat a little wooden foot glider, holding beautiful pink and yellow roses along with a homemade foot rub that would be used when the foot soaks were complete.

Gingerly, Tina dipped her toe into the water. Of course, it was perfect; her granddaughters had made sure of that. The warm, fragrant water felt so good on Tina's tired, aching feet. Whenever the water needed to be warmed up, one of the granddaughters jumped up and topped it off so that she was always perfectly comfortable. Tina was feeling pampered and loved by all those seated with her. Hot herbal tea, sweetened with honey, was served while they sat and visited. The foot soaks were followed by even better foot rubs. Among herself, her daughters, granddaughters and even one great granddaughter, they took turns giving each other foot rubs while singing hymns in German. Many good memories were made, stories were told, and laughter was shared. Tina loved and cherished that wonderful evening. It was the perfect ending to a precious family day.

On another occasion, most of the family was spending time together for one of Henry and Tina's granddaughter's weddings. It was wintertime and there had been a snow storm the day before. The next evening, a couple of Tina's daughters, along with numerous granddaughters, sat outside in the hot tub at Anna's house.

Tina had decided that there was too much snow and ice between the house and the hot tub. Fearing that she may slip and fall, she had decided to stay inside the warm house. While she looked through the glass doors, she saw one or two of the girls hop out of the tub, sit on the ground or lay down to make snow angles in the fresh snow.

One of the girls that had just made a snow angel came running inside.

"Mom, you should tell them that they all have to sit in the snow before they can come inside," she teased.

Just like that Tina open the door and called out, "Before anyone else can come back inside, you all have to either sit or lie down in the snow."

Before they had a chance to respond, she closed the door, turned, and smiled at the daughter beside her.

That's the kind of woman Tina was. Even though she could not join them outside, it did not stop her from joining in the fun.

What a joy it was for the grandchildren to receive their yearly letter in the mail from their grandma!

"You got something in the mail," Anna held up the envelope in her hand, calling to her son as she walked into the house. It was still a couple of weeks until Jacob's birthday but that's exactly the way Tina had planned it. She had done it for so many years and all the grandchildren expected it, so she decided that she dare not be late. She never wanted the children to worry that she had forgotten about them by sending out their birthday gift late.

Toward the end of every year or at the very beginning of the next, Tina would sit down at the table with over fifty packages of gum. It was always the same kind of gum, Juicy Fruit, the kind that came in thin sticks. Tina had found that with that type of gum, she could nicely arrange them and tape them down to fit into an envelope along with a note that she wrote. It was a very small and simple gift, Tina was aware of this. She also knew that if she kept it from becoming overwhelming, she would be more likely to stick to it throughout the years.

The grandchildren enjoyed the gum. It was a fun tradition that Tina had gotten them all used to. The real gift, however, was the handwritten note that was always enclosed. Tina lovingly took the time to write notes of encouragement and blessing to each of the grandchildren every year. Tina's writing was always done in an elegant cursive style that, again, showed her love for beauty and art.

The letters kept coming until Tina simply was not able to hold her pen steady enough to write anymore. She tried hard to keep going, writing only a couple words at a time, steadying her writing arm with her left hand. Sadly, her strength was simply gone. Her hand was shaking as she laid her pen down on the table and, with tears in her eyes, she admitted that she could no longer write to her grandchildren. But there was still one thing that she could do for them. No matter how weak and frail her body became, if God granted her a sound mind, she would pray.

Tina Petkau prayed! It was how she lived. As she breathed, she prayed. And even though she is no longer here, the prayers she prayed for her grandchildren live on. Their impact is not over.

11 LOSING A SON

He pulled his truck up to the front of the family home, hopped out, and ran up to the door. Neither Tina nor Henry could make it to the door in time to greet him, as was their custom. No, today Kris was a man on a mission. He had come to spend time with his mom and, hopefully, help her learn all about using her phone for things other than making phone calls. Texting would be at the top of the list for today.

"Good morning, Mom!" Kris boisterously greeted his mom at the door, removed his shoes, and walked up the four steps to where she was standing, waiting for him. He bent down and gave her a quick hug.

"Good morning, Kristopher," Tina always used his full name. She did not like shortened names. Tina reached up and patted him on the shoulder. "I'm glad you came. It's so good to see you."

They turned and headed toward the kitchen. "The water is still hot from the breakfast coffee," Tina said. "Would you like a cup?"

"Yes, that sounds good," Kris replied. He pulled out a chair from the table and slid it over to the kitchen peninsula, where the remnants of his parents' breakfast sat. Kris sat down and wasted no time in helping himself to a soft chocolate cookie, which was almost a breakfast staple in his mom's kitchen.

"Where's dad?" Kris asked.

"He went out to the shop a few moments ago," Tina replied. "He said he needed to change the oil in one of the vehicles this morning."

She handed Kris a cup of hot water and slid the instant coffee mix over to him. Unless they were expecting company, they didn't bother starting the coffee maker. They preferred to stick to their instant coffee and powdered creamer. She sat across from him and took a sip of her own cooling coffee.

"When do you head out on the truck again?" Tina wondered.

He had started driving a long-distance truck, a few months back, and Tina always liked knowing when he was leaving and where he was going. She had a large map spread out on a table in her sewing area. This way, she could quickly walk over to it and mark the spot that he was at when they had their phone conversations, which happened nearly every day.

"I'm leaving again tomorrow," Kris replied. "Actually, that's why I'm here mom," he continued. "I would like to teach you how to text."

"Oh, I don't know about that." Tina's hesitation was very

evident in her voice and the look that she gave her son. "I don't know if I can or even want to learn that kind of thing."

Tina didn't feel like using her phone for texting. She didn't think that this was something she was up for learning. It was what the younger generation did, not her!

"Mom, it's easy and I really want you to learn to do this," Kris replied confidently, smiling. "Think about it mom, that way you could text me any time you want to. You wouldn't have to wait until I wasn't driving to try to get a hold of me." He had no doubt he would be able to convince his mom.

"Even if you wanted to text me and ask me to call you whenever I got a chance to, that would be cool too," Kris said, continuing with his sales pitch.

Tina sat quietly and listened, trying her best not to instantly shut her mind to the idea. She knew that what Kris was saying was true, and that once she knew how to use the texting feature on her phone, she would find it quite helpful. But it did feel like a daunting task.

Kris slid his chair over beside hers.

"Here mom, can I see your phone?" He reached out his hand and she, reluctantly, gave him her phone. "I'll show you exactly how it's done."

Kris opened her flip phone and showed her how she could text him on her old-fashioned phone, using only the number pad. He was a patient teacher and Tina, very quickly, became an eager learner. She loved the idea of being able to communicate more freely with her son when he was out on the road all by himself. The thought of being able to keep a better eye on his whereabouts was the motivation that she needed to learn to use her phone in new ways.

Learning how to text that day served as an incredible help and blessing in Tina's life. She used it first with her son, Kris, and then it also opened the door to so much more. She was able to communicate with her children and grandchildren in more ways. After a while, Tina became so grateful for the new skill. She knew that because of it she could interact with others in a way that might not have been possible otherwise.

Tina loved all her children equally, but she did have an extra close bond with her son Kris. He didn't have a family to take care of or spend time with, so his relationship with his mom remained more important. On a couple occasions, Kris had told her that she was his best friend.

Tina loved stopping in at his house to visit or to drop off some soup or cookies she had made. His big smile had a way of warming her heart, making her feel special and appreciated. At times, they would sit on his porch or walk around the yard, looking at the different projects he had going on or other things he wanted to show her. In the last years of her life, Tina's hips had been bothering her more. Although she was still sturdy on her feet, Kris, on occasion, would pick her up, lifting her off the porch, and setting her gently on the ground, eliminating the need to walk the three steps.

In April of 2018, Tina was turning eighty and most of their children were coming home to celebrate. What an exciting time! Tina could hardly believe that she was turning eighty. Sure, her body was showing signs of wearing out, but in her mind, she didn't feel old yet. Tina had determined years ago that she wanted to make getting old look good. There were so many stories of elderly people becoming unmotivated, discouraged, or even lazy as they got older. It seemed that in their old age, they wrongly believed their purpose on earth was complete and all that was left for them was to mindlessly pass the time until God would call them home.

Tina knew that this was not the way God had intended for the elderly to live. There was always a purpose and a mission for everyone, no matter their age. So, it was her desire to remain busy for the Lord until her dying day. As her body grew tired more easily and doing physical tasks became harder to do, Tina would focus on prayer. Praying for others was something that Tina was passionate about and something she was able to do while she rested. While she lay awake in bed at night, she would pray. It was something that her aging body would not need to stop doing as long as her mind remained clear and sharp. She was determined to always leave the children with a good impression about old age. She didn't want them to fear the stage of life that she was currently in, but rather look forward to it as a rich and blessed time of life. A stage in life that she happily referred to as *The Golden Years.*

With that in mind, Tina was intentional about keeping her mind active and engaged. She enjoyed doing traditional puzzles with Henry, crossword puzzles, and playing Sudoku. All of these were great mind exercises to help her stay alert and think clearly.

These were the thoughts on Tina's mind as she readied herself for their guests' arrival that day. She got up early that cold but sunny spring morning, expecting a day of happiness and celebration, a day of hugging children and grandchildren as they arrived. Some were coming from Oklahoma, some from Manitoba, and others from parts of Ontario.

She was well prepared, like she always was. Meals had been planned and food purchased. Tina had prepared her customary list of meals for those who would stay at her house. She had then made sure that all the children coming from far away would have a place to spend the night. Some of the relatives would stay at her house, while others would stay at the children's houses nearby. The weekend had been well thought out and prepared. It was going to be a great weekend with the family.

However, the day did not turn out as planned at all. Shortly after breakfast, the phone rang. It was one of her children at the other end, delivering the worst news a parent could ever hear. Their son, Kris had passed away that night. He had been all alone at home when he died. In that moment, Tina knew that her life had been forever changed. That one phone call changed everything. The joy, anticipation, and excitement from just a moment ago was gone, replaced by shock and confusion.

Tina stood, holding her phone in absolute and utter disbelief. How could this be true? She and Henry had gone to see Kris just a couple of days ago. They had sung for him and prayed together. Never would she have guessed that would be the last time that she would see him on this earth.

Her son, who had called her mom and friend, was gone, leaving a gaping hole in her heart and in her life. The tragedy wrapped her in sorrow, leaving her to grieve like no parent should ever have to grieve. Surely this was not how it was meant to be. Parents were supposed to pass before their children, not the other way around.

Without the grace of God, there was no way Tina could have made it through the next days or months ahead. She had gone through many hardships and great difficulties in her life, but never had a pain cut so deep in her heart. The loss of her son Kris was a tragedy, leaving behind a trace of sadness in her spirit that never truly left.

The day of Kris's funeral was deeply sad, but surprisingly beautiful. Hundreds of people came

Tina at her sons' funeral

to say goodbye and to celebrate the life that Kris had lived. He had touched countless people with the way he lived. The stories of his generosity were endless and brought some level of comfort to the hearts of his parents.

Tina's heart broke and shattered in pieces, once again, as she looked lovingly at her son's face for the last time. She couldn't help herself. She gently stroked the side of his precious face. Tears streamed down her cheeks as she wept beside his coffin. How could a mother say goodbye to her child? How could she walk away from him, knowing that she would never see his smiling face again? Never would she hear his voice again or pick up her phone to check if he had texted her. Never again would he say, "Better days are coming." Never again would he hug her.

However, in all her grief, Tina had a steadfast hope and confidence in the goodness of God. She knew, without a doubt, that he was in complete control. Even though she could not understand why things happened as they did, she believed that God had allowed these events to take place and would walk with her through them.

Kris's death had not taken God by surprise. She also knew that one day soon she would see him again. She was not grieving as those who do not have hope. No, Tina had a living hope, a hope that lived in her heart because of Jesus's life, death, and resurrection. Because of Christ's finished work on the cross, they had been forgiven and redeemed, and after this life, would live together with the Lord for all of eternity. What a blessed assurance this gave Tina, to know that saying, "Goodbye", now was only saying, "See you later."

Having her son go on before her as a deposit into God's presence only made the prospect of going to heaven so much sweeter to think about. She thought more of those who had gone before her as well, her precious mother whom she still missed, followed by more and more of her siblings and friends. There were so many waiting in glory already that Tina truly looked forward to the time when she could join them around God's throne. But for now, she would stay busy in this life, doing whatever the Lord wanted her to do.

In the years that followed, Tina continued to pray for many people, many of whom never even knew about it. She would often take a ride with Henry to town and would spend time waiting in the vehicle for him to finish his business. Tina did not pass that time waiting idly or impatiently. No, she prayed for the people that she would see. She said that she had no idea what the struggles or hardships were that they may be going through, so she would pray for them.

It was a joy for her to go to retirement homes with Henry and sing and play their harmonicas for the people there. They would often minister to the people there, many of whom were close in age to them, but who didn't have the health or energy the Petkau's had. This wasn't the only time they would bless people with their actions. When visiting friends or acquaintances in town, they would bring homemade baking or a jar of soup and would pair the visit with some music or prayer.

Tina always made sure to show her appreciation to the doctors, nurses, dentists, and other professionals in her life. She found ways to show kindness to them, while always pointing them to Jesus who motivated her actions. Often after a visit from her, they would receive a freshly made fruit pie or cards of thankfulness and encouragement.

While continuing her prayer, Tina also committed herself to memorize scripture. She knew many songs and hymns, but always placed the most importance on memorizing Bible passages. At this stage in her life, when most people would say they were to old to memorize anything, she memorized the whole *Sermon on the Mount*, Matthew 5-7, as well as numerous Psalms. These were added to a much larger number of verses that she had "hidden in her heart". She would occasionally treat the family by reciting these passages for them, doing it with such expression and feeling, that one couldn't help but see the deep love and respect she had for the Word of God.

12 WELL DONE

This is the part of my mom's story that gets very difficult to think and write about. It is in this last chapter that I will be changing the point of view I write from, as it eventually became impossible to write from my mom's perspective.

It was in the summer of 2019 when we started to notice mom wasn't as strong or healthy as before. Her hips were hurting more, and not being as steady on her feet, she was quite thankful for an arm to hold onto when she walked outside. She said the first time she knew there was something definitely wrong was a day in late August when she bent down to pick up a small bag of potatoes. It was in that moment that something happened to her back. The pain shot through her body and made her wince. It was almost impossible for her to stand up straight with the pain being quite intense. She grasped the hand railing and, gingerly, hobbled up the short flight of stairs, shuffling over to her favorite rocker in the living room.

She sat there for a long while, waiting for the pain to subside. Dad had gone to town, leaving her home alone, but she was expecting one of her daughters to stop in soon. She sat in silence, reflecting on what had just happened. She wondered if something in her back had simply gone out of place or if something was broken. The pain was slowly easing as she sat still and tried not to move.

As she sat there, Mom thought back over the summer. It had been a summer of a lot of aches and pains as well as a great deal of tiredness. There had even been a time when she thought that she may have cracked a rib at the amount of pain on her side. She could feel fear creeping into her heart as she wondered what might be happening to her. She tried to console herself, thinking it was just related to getting older and it wouldn't get worse. She continued to fight her fears and concerns by bringing them to the Lord. She took some time to tell her heavenly Father how she was feeling and what she was worried about. Although the pain didn't leave, her fear did. She settled back into the chair and was able to rest peacefully, knowing the Lord was with her.

For the next couple of weeks, Mom continued having pain in her back and side, a pain that got worse as time went on. Briefly at times, the pain would be almost gone when she sat still or laid down. By the time October came, the pain was truly concerning, and Dad agreed it was time for Mom to go see a doctor. It would have been better to go see a doctor much sooner; however, due to past unpleasant experiences with doctors, Dad didn't see the real need for one, causing Mom to hesitate requesting a visit.

After numerous visits to the doctor, it was determined that my mom had numerous, very painful conditions. Scoliosis as well as degenerative disc disease were seen along with the fracture of six vertebra and a couple of cracked ribs. All these conditions led to the diagnosis of osteoporosis, a bone disease caused by change in bone structure and density.

Mom was sent home with medication that would hopefully deal with the osteoporosis. The treatment turned out to have many bothersome side effects and never felt to help at all. This was very confusing to the family, even for Mom. Seeing others being greatly helped by the treatment became increasingly frustrating to everyone, especially because our mother was the only one who couldn't get better. Other people's bones would mend, causing the pain to go away, but not hers. Ultimately, the pain became so overwhelming that she really needed help finding a way to remove or lessen it. After a couple of weeks at home, she, once again, went to seek medical help.

Dad and a couple of my sisters took her to the emergency room at the hospital in Fort Frances. Sadly, the care she received in the hospital was, to say the least, shameful. Many tests were completed that caused her much pain. She was hardly able to endure the positions requested of her to take the x-rays. Her body was so broken by this point but, she was expected to move this way and that.

At one point, one of my sisters quietly slipped away from mom's side, sneaking into the room where the x-rays were being taken. What she saw deeply concerned her. Having had some medical training, she knew immediately that the bones did not look as they should. There appeared to be countless tiny holes in the bones, somewhat resembling raindrops on a window. Seeing this gave her the sinking feeling that they might be dealing with a type of cancer. Later, when discussing the results of the tests with the doctor, she directly asked if there might be cancer.

"No, no cancer is evident," was the response she got. The only diagnosis they gave was that Mom had osteoporosis as well as arthritis. To be discharged from the hospital, my mom was told she would need to do physiotherapy, as that was apparently going to help her body heal quicker. She would also need to have the house prepared with more railings and numerous other safety features.

The family quickly got to work, installing railings, buying a walker along with other things to make the house safer, easier, and more comfortable for Mom. Christmas was only a couple of days away and Mom really wanted to be back at home. This motivated her to learn the physiotherapy exercises, despite her great pain. She really wanted to be home with her family for Christmas.

We had planned on having our family Christmas gathering at my parents' church in town but plans quickly changed. For mom to be able to rest comfortably, we gathered at mom and dad's house. Many of the siblings had made the drive to be home for Christmas, bringing Mom much joy. This joy was laced with distress since she was unable to serve her children. It was so hard for her not to make food and show hospitality the way that she was used to. Instead, she was confined to her chair or bed most of the time, mostly depending on the help of others.

Seeing mom stay in her chair was difficult for all of us because we knew it was the terrible pain that kept her there. However, Mom was a sweetheart and a joy to be around, no matter how difficult her days were. She was so incredibly thankful to everyone who would do anything for her, making it easy to serve and help her in any way that we could.

When mom was too tired to talk, she would smile at us through her pain. She had the kindest eyes, eyes that could hug her children, and the love she had for her family could not be hidden. Even during her struggle, she filled the atmosphere with peace and joy.

I was so blessed to be able to spend a week at mom and dad's house in January of 2020. It is a trip that I will always cherish. Being able to spend time with my mom that week changed me. We spent hours and hours just sitting together and visiting. She would be snuggled in her special reclining chair, and I would adjust her pillows, blankets, anything to try to get her to be as comfortable as possible.

Next, we would do physiotherapy together. She put in so much effort, believing that it would help her get better. It was torturous! The pain, at times, was almost more than she could bear yet she persisted. When we were done, I would give her a drink of water and lie in bed beside her. She reached for my hand and held it in hers as we cried, prayed, and rested in silence. Those hours with my mom, holding hands and talking about anything and everything, were precious beyond words.

Before mom got up, I would rub her back and tummy. As I did this, I stretched and hurt my neck, which mom noticed right away. In her kindness, despite the pain, she immediately asked for the phone so she could call one of my sisters to come give me a neck rub. She said that she would like to do it herself, but because she couldn't, she had to ask someone else to do it for her. Once again, she was thinking of others instead of herself, despite her pain.

During this time in January, Mom had multiple acute vertebrae fractures, as well as numerous broken ribs. She had another doctor's appointment and this time, it went better than the previous hospital experience. The staff treated her with kindness and thoughtfulness. More tests were done and here it was determined there was an infection present in her abdomen, which would be contributing to her pain. Again, the doctor reassured my mom she was and would continue to get better. He assured her that by summertime, she would be sitting outside enjoying the birds singing and feeling the sun on her face.

My time with my mom was over far too quickly, and saying goodbye that day in January was very hard. I bent over to give my mom a hug, the gentlest hug possible. Her body had become so frail by then. Even the slightest bit of pressure gave her pain. Although I wanted to give her a tight squeeze to say goodbye, I had to restrain myself. I never thought that would be the last time I would see and feel the love in those beautiful, smiling eyes. Had I known this then, I would have stayed a little longer, hung on a little tighter, and thanked her a lot more often. But I had to go, so I turned and walked toward the door. Then I hesitated, turned, and walked back.

"Mom, I just can't go."

I placed my hand on top of hers as I fought hard to keep the tears back. They spilled over and I wiped them away as they rolled down my cheeks. She looked cozy with a soft blanket tucked around her, while her favorite neck pillow was propped up behind her head.

As I walked back toward the door, she lifted her hand, gave a little wave, and said, in a broken voice, "Goodbye, Anna, I love you."

Then, she smiled that beautiful smile of hers, a smile that was meant to comfort me as well as release me to go.

"See you later, mom. I love you!" I called back.

As the weeks passed, Mom was able to do less and less on her own. She was not getting better as the doctors had told us she would. In the back of everyone's mind, I think we all knew that there must be something more serious going on than we were being told, but there were no answers to be found. One of my sisters spent about six weeks living with our parents during this time, while others stopped in frequently to help with whatever needed doing.

By this time, Mom could no longer sleep in bed since the pain from stretching out became unbearable. She had moved into the living room and slept on her reclining chair. One night, after taking a very small dose of morphine, Mom got up at night and wandered around. The next thing she knew was that one of her daughters was standing beside her, both wondering how her walker had ended up at the bottom of the stairs. This experience, along with my mom's strong desire to remain alert and clear in her mind, gave her great apprehension toward taking any pain medication. Being told that she "only" had osteoporosis made Mom think she should be able to bear the pain, without too much medication. She, however, continued to suffer greatly, the only painkiller help she received was that from over-the-counter pain killers. She continued to use these until a couple weeks before she passed away. This, however, only took away the sharpest edge of pain away, never truly riding her of it.

There were still days when Mom would make her way to the puzzle table where she would put puzzles together with Dad. During the past years, Mom and Dad always had a puzzle table set up downstairs, where they would spend countless hours in conversation, putting puzzle after puzzle together. One of my sisters had thoughtfully set up the table upstairs for our parents. Despite this, Dad would often end up sitting at the table alone, and Mom would join him when she felt up to it. At first, she would help by adding pieces to the puzzle; eventually, it became too painful to lift her arms so she would point at pieces she wanted moved with a slight lift of her chin. Then, the time came when she would just sit and watch, but Dad was always much happier with her by his side.

Mom was in too much pain to travel during this time, so a medical appointment was done through a teleconference. Again, the question was asked if Mom had cancer, any kind of cancer? Again, we were deeply troubled and confused when we were told that there was no cancer. Although we were told Mom was going to get better, we could see that she needed more help and care than what she was getting. In March, we were finally able to have nurses check on Mom at home periodically.

My family was heading out on vacation, and I needed to give my mom a call before leaving. She would usually answer the phone in a cheerful voice, but it was different this time. Her voice sounded tired and strained with pain. Her hand was so weak which caused the phone to keep slipping from her ear. I asked her how she was feeling to which she replied, "Don't worry, Anna. I think it's getting a little better every day."

I could not stop the tears as I said goodbye to her that day; I knew that things were not getting better. Mom lived with such strong faith, and she had great hopes she was getting better. She had plans to be sitting outside on the deck enjoying the sunshine and hearing the bird's cheerful song by the time summer came. She was trying to believe what the doctors had said. She was waiting and holding onto the brief hope it might happen.

A few days after our conversation, I received the dreaded phone call that my precious mom was not going to make it. She was in the process of dying. My mind wondered how this could be happening; I knew that people didn't die from arthritis nor osteoporosis.

According to some of my sisters present, our mom had developed intolerable chest pain one night and she had been taken to the hospital. After some testing, the doctor explained that mom had developed pneumonia and because of her advanced cancer, she was only given a day or two to live. That was the first time anyone had heard or been told about Mom having any kind of cancer. For the past few months, she had been fighting multiple myeloma, a very painful and destructive kind of cancer.

With heavy hearts, our family became aware the diagnosis had been in Mom's medical charts for months, yet no one had been told about it. If only we had known what had been going on, Mom's last few months on earth could have been entirely different! There wouldn't have been any physiotherapy, no aversion to pain medication, nothing like that. Because of the pain she was in, Mom was heavily sedated and, over the next couple of days, she was only briefly, able to speak coherently.

God, in his infinite kindness, allowed our mom to see a glimpse of glory while she was still with us. At one moment, an indescribable and incredible joy flooded our mom's being and she started to cry. Danielle was startled and immediately asked what was wrong, concerned that the pain was getting worse.

"No," mom whispered, her face beaming. "My heart is just flooded with joy and peace."

According to my sisters, anything Mom said that day was saturated with thankfulness. It was as if she wasn't fully here anymore but was experiencing the joy and beauty that would soon be hers. From behind her oxygen mask, she was able to tell those present that she loved them, making the effort to look at each person to say, "I love you."

During this time, she heard something no one else could and she was able to tell my sisters about it. She had gazed into the distance and said, "I can hear them, they are calling me by my name already".

Oh, how wonderful it would have been to have been able to hear the people calling her name, as we sat there, wondering who it was she heard. Was it Jesus calling her along with others? I think it may have been her mother and Kris, ready to welcome her into eternal rest. She longed for that rest, to be free from her aching, tired, and broken body. She longed to be free from all the trials of life and to be away from the struggle against sin and evil. Oh, our mom wanted to be at perfect rest.

I was finally able to catch a flight to see my mom. During this time, COVID-19, a virus considered to be highly infectious and dangerous, was entering the scene in Canada and all around the world. Restrictions and rules were changing many times each day, often within the hour. Upon reaching the hospital, I raced inside to go see my mom. I had no guarantee that she would still be with us when I arrived, but at last, I had made it. That is when the ugliness of the COVID restrictions hit me in the face. It was the first day of restrictions at the hospital and I was not allowed to go see my dying mother. I was not allowed to give her a kiss on the cheek and say goodbye. I had not mentally prepared for this to happen and my body went into shock as I realized what was happening. I begged. I pleaded. I was on my knees, weeping in desperation. I needed to say thank-you to my mom, one of my best friends, for all she had been to me.

Moments later, I received a phone call from my mom's room, and someone held the phone up to her ear. I knew she was barely holding on, waiting for all her children to arrive. She did not know what COVID was; she couldn't understand why I was unable to meet with her, given that I was already there. I had told her the day before she didn't need to wait for me but she had waited for me, the last of her children, to arrive. I did not know how to say good-bye. How could I say goodbye to one of the most precious people I had ever known? It was one of the hardest things I have ever done.

During the pain and injustice, God was at work, and we found favor in the hearts of the medical staff. They agreed to honor our request and had my mom released so she could be brought home to spend her last hours with all of us. I got to sit between my mom and dad on that memorable ambulance ride home, the place Mom had called home for over forty years. Although my mom could no longer respond, I was able to have some precious time alone with them.

I talked to Mom of getting home, the place where she could rest and not worry about anything, where she could be surrounded by all her loved ones. As we talked of home, we knew we were talking more about her eternal home than her earthly home. I got to thank her for all she had done, for who she had been in my life, and for being a godly example to me. She had been the first to introduce me to Jesus and had shown me, through her life, that He is worthy of all our worship, praise, and trust. Jesus was her best friend, and now she would soon be with Him. I talked to her of the Grand Canyon and its beauty, assuring her she was going someplace much more beautiful. Then, I said one of the hardest things I could ever say. I told her she could go, that we would be alright. I assured her that all her work on earth was completed, that there was no more she needed to do. She had finished her journey on earth, having lived her life well to the very end. She had been faithful. And then, as if she could truly hear me, she closed her eyes.

Once we arrived at the house, the paramedics graciously set her up in the main area of the house. There, she was surrounded by her husband and all her children, except for one who was there via phone call. Most of our spouses were there along with a lot of the grandchildren. We began our vigil of what we expected to be our last night with Mom, singing and visiting with each other, sitting close to Mom as we held her hands and gently massaged her feet.

A few hours later, our mother went to be with her Savior. She was finally able to gaze upon the face of her precious Lord. What a blessed assurance and perfect hope we have in this truth. Tina Petkau was welcomed into the very presence of the Lord and heard the words, "Well done, my good and faithful servant. Enter into the joy of the Lord."

ABOUT THE AUTHOR

Beverly Wiebe, Tina's youngest daughter currently lives in Texas. She is married to Johnny Wiebe, the love of her life. Together they have two sons, Donnovin and Jared. Donnovin is married to Ana and are expecting their first baby, which will make Beverly a grandma. Beverly gives much credit to her mother, Tina Petkau, for who she has become. She believes her mothers story needed to be told.

Made in the USA
Monee, IL
05 April 2024

55865943R00085